GOD in the DETAILS

Timeless Advice for Christian Womenpreneurs

MARIA TOLLIVER

Dedication

For my baby girl, Jada.

My reward.

My biggest blessing.

My greatest gift.

My Prayer for You

Dear Lord,

Bless the person who is reading this book.

Bless their home, bless their families, bless their finances,
bless their business, bless their health,
bless their spirit, bless their life.

Lord, I pray you will be in the midst of their lives.
Whatever move they make, may they consult you first.
I pray for the families they support;
bless them in whatever they are doing.
Bless their careers and bless their brand.

Finally, Lord, bless their hearts.
I pray their hearts will lead them to Jesus.

I pray that they don't conform to the world and
their business becomes your business.

In Jesus' Name,

Amen

Contents

Are You Called?

*"God created mankind to be managers of what He owns
...and He owns it all."*

~ Dr. Tony Evans

I want to make something clear. I'm not here to tell you how to live your life. I'm not here to tell you how to run your business. I've simply come to deliver a message for the woman who is preparing herself for her purpose. My message is to show you how to walk in your purpose properly as a Kingdom woman and remind you of the position you play in God's Kingdom. *There is much work to be done.*

No, I'm not a minister, pastor, preacher, nor do I hold any title that would warrant me to write such a book. But the content in this book has been weighing heavy on my heart for years. I held off writing it for a long time since I didn't have any of those titles. I didn't feel qualified to write such a book. No matter how many times God called me to write it, I ran from it. Looks like fear, doesn't it? However, through my personal growth and my walk with Christ, I realize that God does not call the qualified but qualifies the called. I hope this book is a helpful resource to you and a reminder of how God's people should conduct themselves in business while walking in their purpose. I will be your biggest cheerleader, cheering you on as you go through each chapter of this book.

You may not like everything I'm going to tell you. It's kind of like the doctor telling you to lay off the salt, and your favorite thing in the world to eat is chips. If you are looking for worldly fluff, there won't be any in this book. I'll be talking about where I think Christians tend to drop the ball. We can find ourselves engaging in things we don't realize are harmful New-Age ideologies and thought patterns that don't serve us well. We sometimes unknowingly have idols in our life, personality glitches we're unaware of, or we take advice from the wrong people. I just want to help you get clear on how to go about pursuing the call God has for you through your business and personal life as well.

Truly, I am no different; I am right there with you. I am just a vessel like you. Even with a bachelor's and master's degree, I am still learning to take myself as being just that—a messenger and manager of what God owns. Are our businesses set up to serve God or not? Are we set up to glorify Him? Or do our businesses look like the world, tending toward self-glory? Controversial topic, I know. But just like any other controversy we give our undivided attention to in our Instagram feeds, we can spare a little attention to this area as well.

In my years working in marketing, I've noticed that Christian business owners and entrepreneurs tend to lean into principles that do not serve God out of fear of what people think. They worry that if we shift away from what makes people comfortable, they won't be successful. My sister, you must remember that success is never determined by a person's comfort level. People are not always going to be comfortable with what you do, and if they are uncomfortable, truth is those aren't your people.

Being successful is not the most comfortable process anyway, so don't let what folks think make you even more uncomfortable. You've got to look at the whole picture.

Listen…

If God gives you a gift, He expects you to use it appropriately.

It's funny how we do whatever we want and then leave out the One who has given us the gifts to be able to do what we do in the first place. Are we doing what we are called to do the *right* way? Have we put the things we need in place to successfully serve God with our gifts and talents?

The Bible repeatedly reminds us that God owns everything in the world. As the Creator, the Scriptures testify to His greatness.

"FOR BY HIM WERE ALL THINGS CREATED, THAT ARE IN HEAVEN,
AND THAT ARE IN EARTH, VISIBLE AND INVISIBLE, WHETHER
THEY BE THRONES, OR DOMINIONS, OR PRINCIPALITIES, OR
POWERS: ALL THINGS WERE CREATED BY HIM, AND FOR HIM."

COLOSSIANS 1:16 KJV

"OUR GOD IS IN HEAVEN; HE DOES WHATEVER PLEASES HIM."

PSALM 115:3 NIV

"YOURS, LORD, IS THE GREATNESS AND THE POWER AND THE
GLORY AND THE MAJESTY AND THE SPLENDOR, FOR EVERYTHING
IN HEAVEN AND EARTH IS YOURS. YOURS, LORD, IS THE KINGDOM;
YOU ARE EXALTED AS HEAD OVER ALL. WEALTH AND HONOR COME
FROM YOU; YOU ARE THE RULER OF ALL THINGS. IN YOUR HANDS
ARE STRENGTH AND POWER TO EXALT AND GIVE STRENGTH TO ALL."

1 CHRONICLES 29:11–12 NIV

God has entrusted you with a purpose to further His Kingdom through
your business. If you own your own home and hire a housekeeper, this does not
make them the new owners. They are just managers of what you entrusted to
them the same way God has entrusted His plans to you. Pastor Tony Evans said
it best, "When you understand that you are not an owner of anything and you're

only a manager of everything that God puts in your hand, it changes how you look at everything."[1]

God created mankind to be His stewards, meaning He created mankind to manage what He owns, overseeing what He has entrusted to us. I encourage you to boldly pursue your purpose without forgetting, most importantly, to use your skills to help protect and expand God's Kingdom. This equation explains how you add to the Kingdom.

PURPOSE EQUATION

God's Plan = Your Purpose + You + Your Skills, Gifts, and Talents

Throughout this book, I will illustrate ways to go about adding to the Kingdom as best I can by shedding light on some big problems in our culture today—idolatry, New Age philosophies, and other tricks the enemy has up his sleeve. We are falling into traps we are not aware of, and it's hurting our witness and God's plans for us. I just want to have a part in helping you uncover some blind spots and understand the areas that trip us up. There's a lot to unpack here. But don't worry—I'm right here with you, praying and cheering you on.

This message is for the Christian business owner, the aspiring "womenpreneurs" who are building something great while trying to find their way. We all have a purpose and should embrace it, study it, and pursue it fiercely. We just need to remember to keep God in the details.

PART ONE

Distractions

"Let your eyes look straight ahead;
fix your gaze directly before you.
Give careful thought to the paths for your feet
and be steadfast in all your ways.
Do not turn to the right or the left;
keep your foot from evil."

Proverbs 4:25–27 NIV

I

Idols

"Idolatry is when loyalty to the creation is greater than your loyalty to the Creator." [2]

~ Dr. Tony Evans

I used to have a very unhealthy obsession with my body. I know most women veer toward this tendency, falling into the comparison trap by comparing their bodies to something they saw on Instagram even when they have bodies the world would deem "perfect." I was never satisfied with my looks, no matter how pretty people told me I was. I was so stubborn and could never take a compliment. Plus, I would always find something wrong with me anyway. *Too fat, too skinny, not curvy enough, too this, or too that.* My obsession eventually led to seeking answers beyond just dieting and exercise. I caught the cosmetic surgery bug, thinking it was the long-term solution that made the most sense. After all, wasn't everyone doing it? Why shouldn't I? If I could have my dream body in less than twenty-four hours, that sounded good to me.

According to the American Society of Plastic Surgeons, in 2019, about $16.7 billion was spent on plastic surgery alone, with about 18.1 million cosmetic procedures performed.[3] I was on my way to being included in that number. I started my journey to find a surgeon and began following a few of them on Instagram. I looked at the reviews and stashed some money aside for it. When I should have been researching marketing strategies for my brand, I was instead researching surgeons. I truly felt that surgery was my only solution to achieve the body goals I wanted; it's all I thought about every day.

The real kicker was when I found out how easy it was to finance the surgery. That's when I became hooked. I also had several friends who'd had work done before, which seemed to turn out well for them. After browsing the many before and after photos of women who'd had the surgery I wanted, then watching videos of how their lives changed, I was convinced it was for me and made my first appointment. It was only a consultation, but I still had to pay a $200 nonrefundable fee. After a while, I started to have second thoughts. I began hearing stories of women who had paid obscene amounts of money, only to have the surgery completely botched. It was a shame, too, as some of them looked even worse than before. Even scarier was that some of them died trying to look more beautiful.

An idol is anything we place a higher value onto than God Himself.

❖

The interesting thing was that I wasn't even looking for these stories. They would just pop up on social media. The Lord was trying to tell me something, and I needed to pay attention. The risk wasn't worth it. I wanted the body but not the surgery. Later, I found out that the surgery would have had me on bed rest for three weeks, and I didn't have the kind of lifestyle or career that supported that kind of time off. Nevertheless, I ended up not going to the consultation, and I never got anything done. I wasted a lot of time with this, not to mention the $200 deposit, which wasn't a whole lot, but it could have been used for something more worth the money. After some soul searching, I realized this obsession with my body had become my idol.

All of us have had idols at some point, or maybe we do right now. We idolize all kinds of things—people, celebrities, money, material things, even ourselves. Yes, we can be our own idols when we obsess over our bodies and appearances. We do this and don't even realize it. Women spend tons of money on hair, skincare, beauty, anything that can enhance our image, and we're willing to break the bank for it. According to statista.com, the revenue of the U.S. cosmetic industry is estimated to amount to about $49.2 billion in 2019.[4]

It gets even worse for black women. In 2018, black consumers spent $54.4 million of the $63.5 million on ethnic hair and beauty aids. Additionally, in 2019, they were in the 79th percentile of mass cosmetic consumers compared to white consumers, who were in the 16th percentile according to Healthline.[5]

Another staggering beauty statistic is that according to salon.com, in 2017, Black women spent $473 million on relaxers, weaves, and other hair care products. Salon.com states this likely occurred partly because of racist ideas that natural Black hair is not professional or attractive. Idolizing our body image can stem from a range of negative projections, like discrimination, mainstream standards of beauty, and trying to keep up with what is culturally acceptable among your peers. These kinds of issues can make any woman feel insecure, causing us to fall into the trap of idolatry.

The word "idol" has several meanings. Merriam-Webster defines idol as "an object of extreme devotion," "a representation, a symbol of an object of worship," or "a form or appearance of something visible but without substance."[6] So an idol could be anything we put our extreme devotion onto, like people, cars, houses, recreation, careers, and so forth. Really, anything we put higher in value than God Himself. We make idols out of many things today, anything that becomes our main source of wellbeing and security, like possessions, money, or even people we don't personally know. There are many, believe me.

In this chapter, we will focus on objects of extreme devotion that trip us up in business and branding. I'm not talking about bowing down to a statue carved out of gold, but whatever we pour our time, energies, and resources into, things like power, people, beauty, money, possession, and attention. Let's look at four idols I've identified that are the biggest influencers and major detractors from our purpose.

ATTENTION

The idol of "Attention" is, in my opinion, the biggest idol of all and a major object of extreme devotion. Becoming obsessed for attention is a trap worse than most addictions and can be one of the biggest distractions from your purpose.

For most of us, gaining attention is a valid goal. If you are a business owner or building a brand, you need eyes on you and your product, but you need the right motives and the right sets of eyes. How you build your business determines what kind of attention you receive. If done incorrectly, the attention you receive could actually be more of a distraction.

Attention-seeking leads to the issue of flattery. I am guilty of becoming a victim of this one. I mean, it can be a tough one to escape, right? As a business owner, the oohs and ahhs in the comments feel really good, but they don't always translate to the business results you're looking for. There are many flatterers out there who love to post a comment but most likely won't buy what you're selling. Be wary of falling into the flattery trap that tempts you by appealing to your pride. Proverbs 29:5 (KJV) states, "A man that flattereth his neighbour spreadeth a net for his feet." Flattery is sweet, but it closes your eyes to the real intentions of the one doing the flattering. Therefore, you cannot see the trap being set.

Getting any kind of positive attention can be very gratifying, but successful people are good at delaying gratification. When it comes to branding and building our business, we want to show the person behind the brand (us) so that our own appearance isn't the focal point. It's hard not to post a pretty picture of yourself sometimes, but delaying gratification comes when we have the self-discipline to keep the posts focused on the brand or business or the services or products we offer. Don't let your Instagram feed turn into nothing but pretty pictures of yourself. There are a lot of influencers out there who get paid a lot of money to grab your attention. They fit this flattery, attention-seeking profile perfectly. They say they are a coach or a consultant of some kind, but all you see on their timelines are selfies and quotes. A selfie or two is ok, but too many screams of someone hungry for attention.

When building our brand, show the person behind the brand (us), not just our own appearance.

❖

If you are building a design agency or career coaching business, you need followers looking for the types of services you offer. People want to see the person behind the brand, but we need to be careful not to make our appearance the brand's focal point. When this happens, you take a detour away from growing an organic following of people in your target market and from what God has called you to do. Remember, you have a huge calling on your life, so don't let the desire to be liked by people become your focus.

Let's be honest. There's nothing wrong with posting attractive pictures, but many of us base our worth on how attractive or funny people think we are. Make it a goal to focus on what is beneficial to your calling by creating content that will help people learn more about the product or service you offer. Maybe you are starting a ministry, have a new book you're promoting, or starting a nonprofit. So, ask yourself, "What do I want the end result to be?" "Who do I want to attract?" If you do the work God has called you to do, the right people will navigate toward you. You get your followers to grow organically by creating content that gives people value (what's in it for them). Learning how to market yourself properly is important and your brand plays a big part in that. But chasing after attention will only take away from that process. Gaining attention is sometimes a necessary evil that can work for you, but it can also work against you, which is why I believe social media has to be both the biggest gift and curse ever created.

If you want to make money, then some attention will be warranted, but you want to get your message in front of the right people with a product or service they are looking for or will in some way benefit them. It's about them, not you!

Attention-seeking becomes a problem when you put yourself out there for all the world to see, and you start receiving all kinds of the wrong attention. This happens when you create content that caters to the wrong people. With social media, Instagram especially, this could be thousands of people at once, which may sound great, but if you have 1,000 followers and only 10% of them engage with you, the 10% are the people who will more likely buy your product or sign up with you. This is hard because who are you most likely going to make content for? The 900 who like your pretty pictures but never engage, or the 100 who comment and click your links? When we allow attention to become our primary focus, we end up leaning towards the 900, but these are the people who are less likely to buy our products. It all gets really confusing. We're not sure who our customer really is. But once we get this concept and lay down our idol of "Attention," we can begin to focus on catering to the people who genuinely want to support us. That's when you'll start to see your ventures really unfold, and things will start to get really exciting for you.

God does not want you to focus on getting attention. He knows your calling and wants you to focus on bringing forth good fruits. So, take some time to revisit your purpose, figure out who your audience is, and how your product will benefit them. God will bring you the people who add value and expose those who do not.

PEOPLE

The idol of "People" is connected to "Attention." People idolatry can involve seeking validation from people or looking up to someone so much that they become the standard for you. These people could be everyone from celebrities to people in your field to certain friends and even family members. Now, don't get me wrong; we need people, and we need each other. Scripture says, "Two are better than one; because they have a good reward for their labour. For if they fall, the one will lift up his fellow: but woe to him that is alone when he falleth; for he hath not another to help him up" (Ecclesiastes 4:9–10 KJV).

God's standard for success is the only one that matters.

We need each other in more ways than one. The problem begins when we look to other people to define what success really is. We look to others for our own validation and security when we should be looking to God, whose standard is the one that really matters. People aren't meant to be worshipped or put up on a pedestal. They crack under pressure and eventually let us down. Here are some key points to remember about idolizing people:

1. We forget that people are human and faulty. We will all fall short at some point, even our most prized celebrities.

2. We use the attention we get from people as a way to measure our success. We need to be willing to do real work to determine how our success is really measured. (We will explore this in more detail in a later chapter.)

3. No matter how tough we pretend to be, we forget that we are human and have feelings. Our feelings are always changing based on external stimuli. Based on that fact alone, you can't put all your faith in people.

4. We forget that we all have expiration dates, which should be enough to keep us from making people into idols. If the fact that we are mortal doesn't humanize us, then, honestly, I don't know what will.

There is always going to be someone more successful, richer, prettier, and smarter than us, so we have to trust we are enough because God says we are. Just think about it. You think this celebrity or influencer has it all together, but what if you were to become them for a week? Would you really enjoy it? Maybe for a while, but I'm sure you would find something about them you don't like.

Finding out what God expects from us and relying on Him to validate us is what's best. I get it. It's tempting to measure success based on likes, comments, what people say about us, and what they *don't* say; however, giving in to that temptation means we put more weight into people's opinions than we ought to. It leads to a tangled web of disillusionment and confusion, and it's not worth it.

The points to remember are this:

- We need to loosen the grip on people, and tighten the grip on God. He won't ever fall short, expire, change, or let us down.

- We can't look to people as the measure for success. God's standards for success looks very different from the world's definition of success. He is more interested in our character than riches or fame or being number one.

- We can't rely on people to validate our worth and security. If we do, we will never be enough— we'll never measure up.

Money

I chased "Money" for years, jumping from job to job just to pay the bills and stay afloat. It was exhausting. I became stuck in dead-end jobs with poor schedules and minimum pay, all because I wanted to see reoccurring money in my bank account. I had little patience back then and couldn't be without a job for very long, so I took whatever gig I could find. As long as it paid above minimum wage, I didn't care. This is a very sad fact on how low my standards were back then. I felt like the only way I could have true peace of mind was by having a certain amount of money in my account to be able to shop, go out to eat, get my hair done, and go on an occasional trip, that's it. Little did I know that idolizing money only got me further away from my purpose. You see, money is the world's currency, but no matter what you do to get it or how much you have, it cannot buy you peace of mind or secure your purpose. For example, when we pray and ask God to help with our financial situations, God doesn't just drop the amount

Idolizing money only gets us further away from our purpose.

we need in our bank account, no. He does provide a way to get it, however.

God requires our participation and to persevere and work hard. If you were just given money on the spot when you asked for it, you could miss the blessings hidden in your perseverance. God wants you to go through a process, one that won't be easy but will be worth it in the end. He wants to see you mature and grow, which is only done by persevering (James 1:4). I'm sure we would all love to have money magically appear in our bank account when we pray, but imagine if God always gave us exactly what we asked for, nothing more, nothing less, just exactly what we prayed for. What condition would you be in today? Do we give everything our children ask for? No, of course not. If we did, what condition would our children be in? As parents, we know best, just like He knows best. In fact, He knows us better than we know ourselves.

"Money" is the one idol that could create a formidable hold on you if you let it. Yes, it has its uses—you need it to exchange for goods and services, etc. But looking for money to solve all of your problems is your first problem. One thing that has helped me with my attachment to Money is trusting God. Of course, this isn't always easy. It took me years, but I found He is the only way I could loosen my grip on "Money"; I had to trust His process, and I would encourage you to do the same. To help you further, here are some actionable ways you can build up your trust in God and remove "Money" as an idol in your life.

- **Practice gratitude.** I usually journal some of the things I'm grateful for, like the people in my life, my health, things like that. I also create encouraging reminders in my phone to go off at random times of the day, like "My life is plentiful with prosperity" or "You are fearfully and wonderfully made." I also recommend downloading the Word Alert app as it gives you daily scriptures. You would be surprised how the Holy Spirit uses this app! It helps to see positivity pop up on your phone when you least expect it.

- **Don't compare yourself to others.** There will always be someone who might be doing better than you financially, and well, so what? You don't know what it took them to get there. Furthermore, never compare your beginning to someone's middle or end. Keep your focus away from other people's pockets and focus on your own. God wants to use you, but He needs your full attention.

- **Create a plan.** Write down what you want and create an outline, even work with a coach if you need to.

- **Work on having a healthy relationship with money.** Create a budget and properly plan for your future. This way, you can control your money instead of letting it control you.

- **Be patient.** I can't stress this enough. Twenty years ago, I was a much more impatient person who jumped from opportunity to opportunity. Slow down; the devil cannot tempt a patient man.

- **Trust God, period.** He is trustworthy and wants good for us.

SELF-HELP

We live in a time where self-help is very trendy; it's all around us. Falling into the self-help trap is something I am guilty of myself, buying self-help books, courses, the whole nine yards. You're probably thinking, *Why is this a problem?* Self-help resources can help you navigate the personal and professional development landscape. That's true. However, these resources can become overwhelming and even *misleading* at the same time. I would listen to every podcast, read every self-help book, and join every marketing webinar I could. I swear I was on every email list, and my Instagram feed was flooded with influencers who claimed to be coaches. I guess you can say I was addicted. I was so motivated and was learning a lot, so I never thought I was doing anything wrong.

Two of my favorite books, classics in the self-help world, are *Think and Grow Rich* by Napoleon Hill and *The Four Agreements* by Don Miguel Ruiz. *Think and Grow Rich* is one of the most talked-about books in the financial literacy world, along with *The Four Agreements* being a prized possession in the world of personal development. Though not faith-based, both books provide timeless lessons that anyone can relate to, many of which I still apply in my own life. The problem was that I became so immersed in them that God's Word became less of a priority. I figured these resources were giving me everything I needed—*I was learning a lot and getting things done, so...?* I should have been using these resources to *complement* my calling, not use them as my foundation.

I got sucked into the self-help movement, and "Self Help" became an idol for me. Also, the packaging of these resources held me hostage—the alluring pictures on Instagram, cute merchandise, business courses, all of that stuff. I loved all the different kinds of journals and planners that popped up during this

*We can take time for self-improvement,
but also allow God's Word to be a part of it.*

❖

movement too. If it was cute and a blush-pink color, I would buy it whether I needed it or not. I guess you can say I was a self-help junkie!

It wasn't long before these self-help books replaced my Bible. Yes, read, take courses, join a mentorship program, but don't let it replace the Word of God—don't let other books and programs become your idol. Take time for self-improvement in *addition* to reading your Bible. For example, if you go to law school, there will be required readings. You may not feel like reading it, but it's for your own good. God also has required daily reading, and it is also for your own good. I don't recommend walking into what God has prepared for you without reading the required reading. I also don't recommend walking in your calling without making your Heavenly Father a part of your daily routine.

Let me illustrate how to achieve this:

1. **Pray.** The Bible says to "pray without ceasing" (1 Thessalonians 5:17 KJV). This means to pray continuously. You don't necessarily have to get on your knees every time, but talk to God often throughout the day.

2. **Read self-help books that align with your beliefs.** You can read self-help books that are categorized as personal and/or professional development but are biblical in nature. For example, *Get Out of Your Head* by Jennie Allen and *Every Good Endeavor* by Timothy Keller are great self-help, purpose-filled books that are Christian-based, written by Christian authors.

3. **Listen to gospel music.** Gospel music reminds us of who God is and brings about a worshipful attitude. You may not think you have time to listen to music, but I would bet there are times in your day when it would work. Sometimes, I listen to gospel music when I work out. Am I the only one who does this? So funny. Yep, sometimes I listen to gospel music when I work out or when I'm out on one of my walks. To my surprise, it suits fitness quite well!

4. **Listen to the Bible, sermons, and podcasts.** Many people work from home or have a commute of some kind. If you can, listen to a sermon or two while you take a work break or while you're driving. When I used to work in an office, my morning drive to work was usually the best time for me to get the Word in. There are tons of Christian podcasts out there where you can find sermons. The one I listen to the most is "The Urban Alternative" with Dr. Tony Evans. The point is to get God's Word in your day somehow.

I just gave some specific steps you can take to make sure *God is in the details* of your routine. Try it and see what works for you. It will become second nature, eventually.

My sisters, we've got to put down our idols. We have to ask ourselves, what is it about that person or thing that makes us use them as our point of reference? What is it that we feel we are lacking in ourselves that makes us idolize other people? Scripture says, "Yet you, LORD, are our Father. We are the clay, you are the potter; we are all the work of your hand" (Isaiah 64:8 NIV).

This verse in Isaiah is one of my go-to verses whenever I feel idols starting to pop back up in my life. It reminds me of who my Maker is. We are all human, so it's easy to get consumed with the world, but our primary source of devotion has to be to our Creator, not His creation. Let's start by putting God back in His rightful place in our lives as our main point of reference and as our primary source for validation. You are who you are because of Him and will become who you are supposed to become if you stick with Him.

2

The Freedom Trap

That thing called freedom. It just might be another idol. We want to be free so bad, don't we? We would do almost anything to be free. I remember my grandmother telling me when I was little that whenever I would see someone leave the house, I would want to always go with them. I would be in tears because I couldn't leave with whomever family member came to visit. I can't remember that far back in detail, but just taking into account the kind of person I am today, that all seems accurate. I always want to leave. I am never satisfied staying where I am. I am happiest when I'm "free."

When I got to be a teenager, being with my friends was one type of freedom, that "I-think-I'm-grown" freedom. My grandma was very strict, so she nipped that attitude right in the bud. She was that "had-to-be-in-the-house-before-the-streetlights-came-on" strict. So whenever I could get away, it felt awesome. I was the only one out of all my friends who couldn't spend the night over at other people's houses unless they were family members. She was a drill sergeant, but I loved her for it. However, my strict upbringing was a big part of why I always craved freedom because I had such limited access to it growing up. I was strictly monitored. If it wasn't my grandmother, it was one of the mothers of the neighborhood. They say it takes a village, and yes, it does.

Back in high school, I would find ways to leave early. Sneaking out and cutting class, you know, typical high school stuff. I even tried to get one of my friends to call and act like my aunt, "Girl, just change your voice a little and tell them it's an emergency." I got caught, but I didn't care; I still left. I lost count of how many times I got picked up by truancy cops. I never wanted to do what everyone else was doing, even if it was right. *God forbid I have to stay in class all day like everybody else!* There just had to be a way out. I eventually found out about this work program that allowed students to leave early to go to work. I talked to my guidance counselor about the program and was able to *legally* weasel my way out of the normal class schedule. I only went to school for half a day.

I guess I wasn't really "free, free" because I still had to go to work, but back then, I thought I was grown; I grew up so fast. So, my senior year, while everyone else was in school until normal school hours, which was around 3:00 p.m., I could legally leave at noon. I had the same classes and sometimes left even earlier to grab lunch. The only thing was, I had to do reports, and my counselor would do site visits to my job to make sure I was really working. I didn't care; I was glad to leave school early and have the freedom I did. The clothing store I worked at was like an urban status symbol or something, so I really thought I was doing something back then. I was happy to have this job; it made me feel grown and free.

As with me and most girls my age back then, being grown equated to freedom. But with all of that freedom, I still wasn't satisfied. Sometimes, my sneaky self would still find a way to leave school even earlier and sometimes leave work early too. I would cut school with some boy or one of my little "grown" friends and go smoke or do something grown, all while ducking and dodging the truancy police. That feeling of escaping felt good, even though I ended up in the back of a cop car several times. I even managed to get my study hall moved to the end of the day so I could have more time to leave. I thought I was so clever.

I'm sure most of us were like this when we were younger—trying to find ways to beat the system. Sometimes it worked, sometimes it didn't. But when you get that first taste of freedom, wow! You want more of it. I hate to compare freedom to a drug, but it can be like that in some ways. Just once isn't enough; it starts to own us. We crave it, even if it leads us away from our purpose or best self.

It felt good riding around the streets, smoking and kicking it with my friends. Your environment is what shapes your perception of what freedom looks like. I wanted to be like some of the fast little girls in my neighborhood who didn't have curfews, dated older men, and were able to run the streets whenever they wanted. That was a type of freedom I wanted, too, with no parental supervision. No matter what form freedom comes in, we all want to be free in some way. It's natural to want to be free—freedom is in our DNA—but there is a difference between our own personal freedom and the freedom God has for us. That's what this chapter is about.

Why I Became an Entrepreneur

There are some things you can't put a price on, peace being one of them and freedom the other. You could never pay me enough to have either of those things taken away from me. I was in love with the idea of being free, especially when it came to my career. Entrepreneurship seemed like a no-brainer to me, being able to set my own schedule and work when and where I wanted to. Who wouldn't want that? It's possible the freedom that comes with being an entrepreneur is very alluring to you and has something to do with you wanting to start a business in the first place. Freedom is very attractive to many of us and, unfortunately, sometimes takes the place of our calling. We'd rather be free than walk in our calling. I, along with everybody else in this entrepreneurial revolution, decided long ago to start my own business for two main reasons—financial freedom and flexibility. Sure, I love to write, and there's no doubt that writing is my calling, but other than that, I wanted to be financially free. I never thought of any other reason why I wanted freedom so bad other than a better work-life balance and not having to worry about being a corporate punching bag.

I had to be an entrepreneur by any means necessary! That was the mindset I had. I was tired of working in call centers, so I didn't care if I was pursuing my calling or not. I was desperate! After so many failed attempts trying to find work in my field and always falling into the call-center trap, I became obsessed with entrepreneurship and the freedom that seemed to come with it. I swear, I followed every coach, took every course, read every book, downloaded every podcast—I just went crazy trying to learn how to succeed on my own. It wasn't that I wanted to be an entrepreneur; I felt like I *needed* to be an entrepreneur. I needed to work for myself. I felt like I would continue to be stuck if I didn't. I needed to be *free*.

Many people probably feel that way, but it feels even more urgent when you are a creative person, like myself. I don't know how it is for non-creatives, but for us creatives, we need stimulation. We either need to be working in our field of choice or working for ourselves, period. If we try to do anything else, we go crazy. We have to create, write, or design something, or we'll lose it.

If we can't find a job doing what we love, the next thing would be to start our own thing. That was me. If I couldn't find a job in my field, I would have to use my talents to start my own business or end up back to call-center land. That's what I did, since I carry two very creative degrees, which are either too creative to find a job, like Cleveland where I'm from—there is virtually no creative industry there, or there's too much competition, like in Toronto where I moved to—there are too many creative people there. I was either overqualified, had too much competition, or companies didn't see my creative skill-sets as relevant. Whatever, it was their loss. If you have a creative degree and can't find work in your field, then you could pretty much end up in a cubicle with a headset as a leash unless you do something about it.

The thought of working a dead-end job was terrifying to me. I started to crave entrepreneurship, the whole work-from-anywhere lifestyle. What would it look like? Maybe I'd work in my pajamas or on the beach with a martini in my hand. It looked so good to me; it was an escape, so I made that my goal. This lifestyle was so attractive. I mean, everybody was doing it, *everybody*. All you saw were the pretty posts on Instagram with their feet in the sand and a cute sundress promoting some course they created. With all the cute inspirational messages and all the eye-catching colors in my feed, it just intensified my pursuit even more. I knew a lot of that stuff was staged, but hey, they still made it look so good. All you needed was a laptop, wi-fi, and basic content creation and administrative skills, and you were all set.

Well, shoot! I have both and then some. I'm talented, got two degrees, tons of experience; I would blow this out of the park. How could I not do this? I would tell myself, *Maria, you have to do this, I mean, this is what you're called to do! You got the skills, the talent, and the money to start, just go for it,* and that's exactly what I did. I bought my domain, got my social media together, and my automated email campaigns going. In not too long, my freelance marketing agency was born. I really thought this digital nomad lifestyle was my calling. I even joined Facebook groups and paid for courses. I was going to make this work by any means necessary. Who wouldn't want to be living it up in Bali or Jamaica sipping tropical drinks while working on their laptop? This sounds like a dream to most people, especially to the front-liners or corporate punching bags of the world. I'd done it all—call centers, retail, sales, desk jobs; you name it. I was ready! I would do anything to get out of this routine. Sign me up!

The "By-Any-Means-Necessary" Effect

Freedom is thrown around a lot these days—financial freedom, freedom of speech, free will, free products and services, and so forth. I wanted all of this by any means necessary. The financial freedom and the flexibility to do whatever I wanted when I wanted was my primary motivator, nothing else. With that mindset, I leaned into resources and people who validated this kind of freedom. I always knew that writing was my calling, but I didn't pursue it. Instead, my main focus became designing the life I wanted for my husband and me to be free to move about the cabin. Maybe after I accomplish that, I would focus on writing.

We'll do anything to be free, won't we? We will delay our calling just to get our freedom fix. Being free feels good, but we cannot just focus on freedom. Even in our businesses, we want to do what we want to do to achieve this freedom instead of doing what we need to do to achieve God's will for our lives. That's what happened to me. My pursuit of "freedom" distracted me from my true calling and purpose.

God's freedom may require you to give up your personal freedom for a time, but it's totally worth it.

God's purpose for you is much greater than your freedom fix. I heard Him say to me, *"Stick with me, and I'll give you a freedom that's sustainable, not this quick, fly-by-night freedom you keep pursuing."* If you stay consistent with God's will for your business, your reward will be much greater than just freedom. His plan for you is not a fix; it's guaranteed to last. If God gives you a gift, He gave it to you for a reason and expects you to use it accordingly, not just so you can be free. Our issue is that our desire to be free distracts us from our true purpose, and we fall for it every time. Choose freedom, but choose *His* freedom. God's freedom may require you to give up your personal freedom for a while, but honestly, what He can offer in place of that is totally worth it. His calling for your life needs to be the motivation behind you using your gifts and talents, not just this whole freedom thing. Freedom is not without its obligations.

People forget that you have customers, clients, and employees to show up for with entrepreneurship. The reality is, in some ways, entrepreneurship can be even harder. You don't have a promised paycheck coming your way, so it's up to you to make it happen. *Basically, you gotta earn it.* You have the freedom that comes with running your own business, but you have the responsibilities too. *That's the part we seem to forget.* Enjoy the perks of entrepreneurship, but don't take it for granted. Don't be focused only on the freedom.

STEWARDSHIP

> *Steward: a person who manages another's property or financial affairs; or to manage or look after another's property.*[7]

I talked a little about stewardship already in the introduction, but there is so much to say about stewardship and the freedom it gives us when we do it well. We are managers of God's affairs and His Kingdom down here on earth. Ultimately, we are to use our skills and talents to manage what God gives us to advance His Kingdom. We cannot fully claim ownership of anything, not even our own businesses. I know you're probably thinking, "But, it's mine. I built it!" Yes, it's your business, but you cannot take all the credit. Stewardship is a managerial responsibility, not ownership, and forgetting that will always create conflict.

God has given you a set of skills that you are free to use to serve Him and others. You will hear me speak about stewardship often in this book because we need to learn the part we play in God's Kingdom. First Corinthians 4:1–2 (CSB) says, "A person should think of us in this way: as servants of Christ and managers of the mysteries of God. In this regard, it is required that managers be found faithful."

I can count on one hand how many times I've heard people speak about stewardship. I don't think I've ever heard the word uttered more than three times in my life, except maybe at church. But folks, it is not just a religious term. At least it shouldn't be confined to that category only. God has appointed you to be His *faithful* manager, which involves how well you manage your purpose. I want to make sure you're not getting caught up in just having freedom because, really, the freedom you want is tied to your purpose. It's not a sin to live a dream lifestyle where you're your own boss, but regardless, you should always be about your Father's business. Who knows, that work-from-anywhere dream lifestyle might be in God's plan for you somewhere down the line. *Wouldn't that be amazing?* You just have to keep living and trusting that what God has for you is worth pursuing.

A big part of stewardship is building ourselves up so we can free others. *What? To free others, why is that?* The whole point of your purpose, no matter what, is to serve others—customers, patients, clients, suppliers, including our families and friends. We are all in the service industry, no matter what we do, whether we work from home or on the beach. God's process is always about getting us set up to serve others while fulfilling His Kingdom agenda, which could ultimately lead to the freedom you are trying to achieve. I'm not trying to tell you to give all your time away; no, just trying to get you thinking like a steward. It never really occurred to me to use my freedom to help others for a long time. I mean, you couldn't tell me that growing up.

There is freedom in freeing others.

Let's say you've finally achieved your dream of entrepreneurship, walking out those corporate doors, never to look back. You have your laptop, and your home office looks Instagram-ready. You did it, girl; *you're finally free!* Not only are you your own boss, but you also have more time to spend with your family, more time for self-care, and the freedom to design your life the way you want it to be. But wait—you're still a steward. When I started working for myself, I started doing anything I wanted to do—traveling more, dining out more, and my social life was envious. I lived an overindulgent lifestyle for a long time, going out every weekend, going to brunch on Sundays instead of church, dining out several times a week, sometimes twice a day—it was crazy. Pretty much any money that came in went right back out to my social life. I admit I was being selfish.

You see, the issue with having too much freedom without a good sense of stewardship is that we get the freedom we pray about and fill it with our own stuff. Using our time to serve others is what God has called us all to do; it's what stewardship is all about. We can't just hoard our gifts and blessings to ourselves. We are leaving a lot of souls on the table when we do that.

In addition to using our God-given gifts as Christians and stewards, we all share a common responsibility to tell people about Jesus. Yes, Jesus! In some way, shape, or form, we need to be sharing the gospel. This may not be the most comfortable thing to do, but your status or position does not exempt you from evangelizing. All Christians, all of the saints, no matter what role you play in society, your role in God's kingdom is much bigger. Remember, we are all stewards. Now you got the freedom; well, don't leave Jesus out of it. Don't let your pride in who you are get in the way of doing God's work. Your status is one of those things that the enemy can use against you if you're not careful. Whether you're an entrepreneur, celebrity, influencer, politician, or public figure, in some way, you need to be sharing the gospel of Christ.

I know that mixing religion with business and personal affairs can be tricky, but you let God worry about that. Continue to be a good steward. You have to understand that everybody will not like your message, but that doesn't mean you keep quiet. I've spent a lot of time in prayer about this very topic. Let's say you are high enough in the ranks of society, maybe a politician or a public figure, and you might have access to a type of freedom that the average person wouldn't have. You could be using your freedom to be a voice for people who don't have a voice. Maybe you have access to millionaires, celebrities, or important political figures. *Just imagine what would happen if you brought Jesus into all these circles!* The problems you would solve, the type of shield you would create would be unbreakable.

I jumped from job to job because I didn't allow God's plan to come to fruition until much later in my life. If I wasn't getting something from a job, I would move on to another. I would stay at some jobs for only a few months; I even worked four jobs in one year—not very proud of that. I never thought any company was worth it enough to stick around for longer than three years. All these corporate environments were the same to me, but I still felt like the next one would be different.

I chased freedom for a long time, for too long. That feeling was addictive. You see, this is where we go wrong. We chase after a feeling instead of a solid foundation. It's the difference between God's freedom and our own personal freedom—we need to know the difference. I look back now, and wow! I could have been working and walking in my calling a long time ago! But I was so busy chasing these little "freedoms" and false senses of security that I couldn't see the bigger picture. I had a very narrow view of what freedom was. I would kill for anything that gave me weekends off, believing that traditional nine-to-five

Do you want to be free?

schedules would make my life easier. I would settle for scraps when God wanted to give me the main course all along—His long-term freedom that was attached to my calling as a writer.

Why do we do this? As humans, we are impatient and always need to be in control. That's why we run away or settle and twist and turn and do whatever it takes to achieve the freedom we think is best for us. This whole process has become something we normalize. I am a writer. I've always been a writer, so I know good and well I wasn't supposed to be working in retail and call centers, but I was too impatient, and they hired quickly. I needed money fast to eat, pay bills, shop, and have a social life. I wasn't thinking about the big picture; I just needed something, anything that was easy to get so that I could hold on to these little freedoms I wanted. I sold out for far less than what God had for me.

Stay the course. If you do this and don't keep disrupting your flow, you'll get there. One big problem I had was that I would pray and ask God to help me find a job, *"Lord, please help me get out of this job, that job, help me, please find something, help me, help me, help me!"* See, I wasn't praying correctly. I was asking God to keep me in this cycle, and well, that's exactly what happened, so be careful what you pray for.

I should have asked God to reveal to me the steps I needed to take to achieve what *He* had for me. *Lord, where do I start? What connections do I need to make? What kind of things should I write about? Lord, help me find a mentor, order my steps.* Those are the questions I should have been asking, but I was always thinking about a faster way out. Later in life, I found that had I allowed God to order my steps in the beginning, I would have been blessed with permanent freedom—God's freedom, not these short-term "freedoms" I kept pursuing.

With that said, do you want temporary freedom or permanent freedom? For me, I wanted the latter, and I have never looked back since. I am now thriving in my writing career, have made lifelong connections, and am using my degrees in ways I never thought I would. This book would have never happened, nor would I have a successful writing career had I not pursued my purpose. I look back over my life, like wow, the freedom I wanted was always attached to my purpose. So, do you really want to be free? Your choice, so choose wisely.

3

Bad Advice

SUNFLOWER, MISSISSIPPI

Like most black families, mine is from the South; Sunflower, Mississippi, to be exact. My family's history began as a farming family rooted in extremely humble beginnings. They grew up on farms, grew their own food, drank their water, and minded their business. They are as Southern as it gets and could tell you a thing or two about hard times. They didn't put up with any nonsense, either. I remember my grandmother telling me that her mother (my great-grandma) would be perched up on the front porch with a shotgun. I mean, hey, *it was Mississippi in the 40s*. My great-grandma had eleven siblings—three sisters and eight brothers, and she had eleven children too. My grandmother told me she was trying to get twins, but she gave up after ten. Things were hard yet simple.

I would be the first to tell you that the advice you get from your elders is timeless and suits whatever issue you're going through. My dad and grandfather would always tell me to "never count your chickens before they hatch." My family has always been a "don't-believe-it-till-we-see-it" kind of family. My grandfather told me to never cosign for anybody, and out of all the advice he's ever given me, that one stuck for sure.

One thing my grandma used to always say was, "A hard head makes a sore butt!" If I heard her say that, it meant a whooping was right around the corner. She certainly has tons of catchphrases, as I'm sure most grandparents do. When I got older, she would still say it but apply it to different issues. There is nothing like that good ol' Southern old-school advice—straight to the point but packed with good knowledge. My grandma used to tell me, "The devil has power but only the power God allows him to have." That always gave me hope because

Give cheerfully, don't stuff yourself, and don't worry.

that reminded me God is always in control. He always has the final say, and the standard would always be lifted.

My grandmother is also the most giving person I know. If you came to our house, you would always leave with a care package. I remember growing up, there would always be bags packed with all kinds of stuff we thought we didn't need. *What are all these bags for?* They were for visitors! Whoever visited the house would get a bag. It would be filled with all sorts of stuff, from air fresheners to cleaning products. She couldn't help it—she loves helping people; it's her gift. Whatever she thought someone needed, she would give it to them. In her eyes, you never know what people might need. It's funny how, later, I eventually did find a use for the things she would give us, like all the paper clips, rubber bands, and other random things. I always wondered, how is this eighty-something-year-old woman in better health than most younger people? Heck, she might be in better health than me! It took me a while, but I figured it out—it's because she gives. One of her favorite scriptures to quote is from 2 Corinthians 9:6–7 (ESV):

> *"Whoever sows sparingly will also reap sparingly,*
> *and whoever sows bountifully will also reap bountifully.*
>
> *Each one must give as he has decided in his heart, not reluctantly*
> *or under compulsion, for God loves a cheerful giver."*

I had been doing some thinking, and three things stuck out about my grandma. She never worries (I've never known her to have anxiety about anything), she gives, and she eats like a bird. This is why she is as healthy as she is, and why she's never had more than a cold as long as I've known her. She would always tell me, "Maria, stop worrying! Don't you know God's gonna handle it?" Sometimes I have to be reminded of the God I serve.

Just imagine what your life could be like if you stuck to simple advice. Give cheerfully, don't stuff yourself, and don't worry. That's my grandmother's advice in a nutshell, and I'm extending that same advice to you. She is a living breathing example of 2 Corinthians 9:6–7. She gives cheerfully, and you know what? God has blessed her with good health.

My family has always been my first point of contact when I'm going through something. We all go through challenges and adversities, so we all need sources of good advice to help us steer clear of sources of bad advice. Advice from people who live simply and have been through a thing or two can be very valuable.

You vs. the Enemy—Choosing Your Sources

"WHETHER YOU TURN TO THE RIGHT OR TO THE
LEFT, YOUR EARS WILL HEAR A VOICE BEHIND YOU,
SAYING, 'THIS IS THE WAY; WALK IN IT.'"

ISAIAH 30:21 NIV

Filtering out all the noise can be the challenge of a lifetime. It is a moment-by-moment check and balance. Most bad decisions come from not being able to filter out distractions. For a long time, I got sucked into all of this women's empowerment stuff. There's so much of it out there, and it's easy to get lost in it. We've got so many social media influencers claiming to have it figured out, but really, everybody is singing the same song, just packaging it differently. *So, who do you believe?* I've bought courses and sought mentoring from people I later found were so far from my values. We all make these kinds of decisions, but the more you spend time with God, the easier it will be to hear His voice amidst all the noise. Your vision will become clearer, and you will begin to choose your sources more wisely. This is exactly what the devil doesn't want—he doesn't want you to have clarity.

You are supposed to be something great—something powerful, and the enemy is aware of this. John 14:12 (KJV) says, "Verily, verily, I say unto you, He that believeth on me, the works that I do shall he do also; and greater works than these shall he do; because I go unto my Father." Don't you want to know what these greater works are? Do you know who doesn't want you to know? The devil. It's true. Our adversary, the devil, doesn't want us to win and will do everything he can to keep us from moving forward. He will tempt us with things that appear valuable but are not. Next thing we know, we'll have "shiny object syndrome." This is why discernment is so important, and why we need to know what we are up against.

"FOR WE WRESTLE NOT AGAINST FLESH AND BLOOD, BUT AGAINST PRINCIPALITIES, AGAINST POWERS, AGAINST THE RULERS OF THE DARKNESS OF THIS WORLD, AGAINST SPIRITUAL WICKEDNESS IN HIGH PLACES."

EPHESIANS 6:12 KJV

You can't walk into your purpose blind-sighted, so you must know that thing is deeper than what you see in front of you. The spiritual battlefield is very different from the physical so you have to know how to fight. You need to vet your sources, obtain the right information, and have the right people around you.

The enemy hates that you are going after your purpose. He hates that you have a purpose in the first place. He hates that you are starting a business, and he hates that you are being a boss. Yes, he hates that you have goals and dreams, but I do know one detail he likes—bad advice.

*Vet your sources, obtain the right
information, and have the right people around you.*

Information

Information is one of the enemy's favorite tools, and since there are already so many corrupt sources out there, it just makes his job a whole lot easier. That is why I'm so particular about where I get my information from, and so should you. I remember watching an interview with Denzel Washington, and recall him saying, "If you don't read the newspaper, you're uninformed; if you do read the newspaper, you're misinformed."[8] So, what do we do?

Everybody has something to say these days. Everybody is an expert, a coach, a teacher—everybody is somebody. We all have assumed some type of title to make what we say more relevant than the next person. All this does is pose too many solutions to the same problem and too many roads to the same destination. It's great that we are coming up with our own solutions and making things official by creating personal brands and starting trends—we even made the term "influencer" an actual job title. *You couldn't ignore it anyway; it took on a life of its own.* The problem is, there are just too many competing sources out there, so you have to narrow down where you're getting your information from. We've got too many outlets and too many people claiming to be influencers when they are really just ambassadors of their brands. All information is not beneficial; some of it is just flat-out noise.

The Media

Most information comes from the media or *weapons of mass confusion,* as I like to call it. I think the media is one of the enemy's favorite weapons to use. The sad part is that the media is not all bad. There are some reliable sources out there, but unfortunately, those get overshadowed by all the nonsense. People fall victim to this every day. I've had to wean myself off checking Apple News every day. I used to be sort of a news junkie just as much as I was a self-help junkie. At the same time, I had a bunch of news accounts I followed on Instagram. Everywhere I turned, there was the news, and never really good news, either. If I wasn't watching it, I was being notified about it. Do you know what I did? I turned those notifications off! The Instagram notifications too. And when I found out I could mute accounts on Instagram, I did that as well. Let me tell you, the peace of mind I got from doing that felt incredible. The way I started looking at it is, if something was going on and it was important enough, I'm sure I would find out about it. You must protect your peace, people!

My suggestion is to pick five reliable sources:

- One that serves your community
- Another that serves your industry (your business or whatever you do for a living)
- One for self-care
- One go-to for entertainment (we're human; it's good to have a laugh every now and then)
- One that serves your faith, in addition to the Bible. Examples of popular Christian outlets I like are "Relevant Magazine," "Christianity Today," and "Sojourners."

I know it will be hard. I mean, you can find at least thirty for entertainment! The point is to limit your sources. You don't need to consume content from ten different news sources to find what you're looking for. I don't think we realize how much time we take up consuming all this. Protect your peace, sanity, and your time, which is also very valuable.

Discernment

Discernment will be the most helpful skill in vetting your sources. I don't want you to miss this because this is where the enemy has his claws in a lot of people. *Remember, he is the master of confusion and illusion, but having discernment will help you expose him.* Discernment will be one of your best weapons of choice because it is the final determining factor of what's right and wrong. The way I look at it is right is right and almost right is still not right, *and if it ain't right, then it's wrong, period.* If you get an answer almost right on an exam, nine

It's either right or wrong, no grey areas, no matter what kind of spin the world tries to put on things.

times out of ten the teacher is still going to mark it wrong. There have been times when I've had teachers give me a half-point, but there are no half-points in the real world; almost just won't cut it. It's either right or wrong, no grey areas, no matter what kind of spin the world tries to put on things.

One way to practice discernment is through prayer and fasting. Fast regularly and be intentional when you pray. Fasting could be giving up food for a few hours (if you can do that). Most people pick one day out of the week and fast from 6:00 a.m. to 6:00 p.m., no food, only water during that time. The most I've fasted was a week, and it was very effective. I kid you not, so many doors opened for me. Things just clicked into place! Even things I didn't ask for, I received.

In addition to fasting, you can advance your discernment by staying in the Word daily, something I can't stress enough. I downloaded an app called Word Alert that sends me Bible verses every day. It gives me daily encouragement and reminds me to pick up my Bible and get spiritually fed. God's Word is one of the biggest tools you have in increasing your discernment outside of prayer and fasting. It is the last piece of armor listed in the Armor of God from Ephesians 6:10–18. Other than that, you just need the one thing that ties it all together, faith.

Reading

Read as much as you can. Don't rely on social media for all your information. I was born in 1984 and grew up in the 90s, so all we had were books, magazines, and television. We didn't have social media or smartphones, so that eliminated two big outlets right there. While I was building my brand, one of the most inspiring books I've ever read, hands-down, was *The Alchemist* by Paul Coelho. *The Alchemist* is the perfect blend of fiction and inspiration. That book taught me more about personal and professional development than most self-help books. Read books that add value and are recommended by people you trust.

Mentors

Next, find a mentor. For the longest time, I thought mentorship was just for kids, but the fact that Oprah, Diddy, and even Steve Jobs all had mentors proved me wrong. I ended up hiring a coach, and I wish I had done it sooner. Even one of the richest men in the world, Warren Buffet, had a mentor by the name of Benjamin Graham, author of *The Intelligent Investor.* I would encourage you to find someone more knowledgeable than you are in your field. Also depending on what stage you're in, most people won't mentor you until you've got something to work with, so keep that in mind. I would encourage you to seek out a mentor. Find someone you can trust, who has been where you are and doesn't mind showing you the ropes. We should have at least one person we can confide in with our dreams and business plans.

Mind Your Business

Have you ever thought that you might not need *any* advice right now? Keep building and minding your business, and you might just get somewhere. You might not know what you're doing yet, but keep building your foundation so you're able to apply the advice when ready for it. I used to have a problem with trusting myself, which caused me to develop imposter syndrome, something a lot of women deal with. I researched and looked for advice everywhere on this "syndrome," which was a new term at the time. There were even multiple celebrities that talk about experiencing this, like Tracee Ellis Ross and even the First Lady Michelle Obama. The fact of the matter is, after reading these sources, they always ended up leading me back to myself to figure it out. So, after a while, I just stopped researching. I prayed about it and continued to build my foundation, using the intuition God gave me. You don't always need someone to verify for you what you already know.

Sometimes we can lead ourselves to unnecessary detours, which is why you shouldn't share your problems with everyone—just mind your business. This is another way you protect your peace. Only share with like-minded people who can relate to your experiences, giving you a more valuable support system. We all need help but help from the *right* people. We've got businesses to build, communities to empower, and generational curses to break! I don't even waste my time talking to people who aren't about much, and you shouldn't either. If they don't add value, then you truly don't have time for them.

Good Advice

As crazy as this world is, good advice does exist. There are still some people out there you can trust. You just need to dedicate some time to sort through them. Look at it as an interview process. When companies are looking for someone to hire, they check their resume and look for certain skill sets. Then, if they like what they see, they call you in for an interview. If that goes well, they usually check your references. If you make it past that, then you'll get a background check. If that checks out, then most likely you made it. Now, do the same thing when looking for a mentor or coach. Some of them really are legit, and if you are serious enough about your goals, you will take the roads you need to find the right person. Find out their credentials—do they have any testimonials? What kind of content do they post on social media? Do your own background check on them.

Another thing you need to do is put your pride aside. There is nothing wrong with asking for advice, and there is no room for pride when trying to build a business or a career. There's no room for pride when building *anything*. Some people would rather stay stuck than ask for help, and that's not going to be you. There will always be consequences in your comfort zone, remember that. The help is out there; we just need to put in the effort to find the right kind of help. Bad advice is everywhere, but good advice is not so visible. Most importantly, always measure any advice you get with the word of God and see how it holds up. If you are looking for a coach or influencer, make sure they are truly God-fearing. I would hate for you to get advice from someone who isn't and they lead you right into the enemy's trap. This is why discernment is key. Everybody is not going to identify as a Christian, but I can't rock with people who don't respect godly principles. To clarify what I mean, let me share an example.

There was one influencer I used to follow, who I admired. For the sake of privacy, I will call her Lisa. I loved her vibe and her brand, and I even considered going to one of her events. There was one podcast where she was interviewing another influencer (I'll call her Sarah), who is an entrepreneur, author, Christian, and someone I also admired. You could tell she was a God-fearing Christian by the way she spoke with confidence about her testimony, and what I loved was that she wasn't shy about defending the gospel either. To be honest, she was too real for this podcast. I love how she answered perfectly these interrogating-like questions that challenged her faith.

Lisa really tried her, challenging her faith, questioning why she would go so hard for something that people might be uncomfortable with. The thing about this is, Lisa believes in God. She quotes Him often, but that's about as far as it goes. Therefore, the fact that she would devalue the Bible wasn't surprising, and it bothered me. You don't have to be a Christian for me to listen to your podcast, but the minute you start devaluing Scripture and talking down on Christian principles, I'm no longer interested. This attitude of undervaluing the word of God is all too common among influencers today. All I could say was "wow"; it was hard to listen to this podcast after a while. It was like she was trying to get Sarah to give in, but true believers never give in. Sarah made sure that Lisa knew whose side she was on, and that side was Jesus'.

Lisa really put a bad taste in my mouth. Not long after that podcast, I deleted Lisa's podcast and started listening to Sarah's podcast. I always wondered why I would see Lisa post about God but never quote Scripture. It was because she doesn't believe in it. Like a lot of New Age influencers, they quote God all day but don't believe in Scripture. Throughout that podcast, she was denouncing biblical principles, and I just couldn't sit through any more of that. Even though she did share beneficial information and dropped a gem every now and then, still, after that I was done with her. I didn't even need much discernment for that; my spirit just wouldn't allow me to consume any more of her content. When you get to a certain point in your relationship with God, your taste in things will change and your taste in people will change, too. You will start to crave direction from people who swing the same way you do.

Where I'm at now in my spiritual journey, I could never take advice from someone like Lisa; it just wouldn't work for me. We all have our preferences of who we choose to counsel us, but my loves, you must be very careful who you let pour into you. Research them, listen to them for a while, and most importantly, see how they treat other people. I am very cautious about who I let in my circle. Even my Instagram feed looks different than it did a week ago.

THE NEW AGE TRAP

Watch your step, sis, it's a trap—a BIG one. The New Age movement weighs heavy on my heart because it especially affects women. This is where your discernment is going to have to be on point. New Age spirituality is a whole book in and of itself, but I would be remiss if I went without mentioning it in

'A lot of New Agers think Christians aren't "woke," but I'll tell you, I've never been more "woke" in my life.

this one. A lot of advice these days stems from New Age beliefs. I swear, New Age culture really frustrates me because it gives more credit to creation than the Creator. New Age spirituality formally defined represents a variety of persons who have cut ties with the dominant capitalistic and Judeo-Christian beliefs of late-twentieth-century America. These are people who take part in redefining spirituality and the natural order of things, like gender, marriage, physiological makeup, and everything that defines humans and society. That's the formal explanation. In other words, it's a movement that has redefined Christianity by mixing worldly views with Christian views of how one should operate spiritually. The New Age movement is thought to be a more progressive form of spirituality, viewing biblical beliefs as "old school" or "a thing of the past." A lot of New Agers think Christians aren't "woke," but I'll tell you, I've never been more "woke" in my life.

In New Age society, everyone is liberated, free, and empowered enough to where they feel they don't need God for anything. They only stick Him in the parts they see fit. It's a complete misuse of free will, something God gave to us in the first place. Therefore, He still expects us to be obedient, which means not conforming to the world. Romans 12:2 (KJV) says, "And be not conformed to this world: but be ye transformed by the renewing of your mind, that ye may prove what is that good, and acceptable, and perfect, will of God." The word "conformed" means to agree with or match something,[9] but "transformed" means to change in composition or structure.[10] When transforming, you become a new creature, but when you conform, no change is made—you are just complying. When you engage in New Age practices, you are complying with New Age principles. You might say, "Well, I don't engage in such practices," but the thing is, you may not know you are.

Crystals and Other Tools

Probably one of the most popular tools used in New Age spirituality, and possibly the most popular among millennial women, is the use of crystals. A lot of people don't know this, I was unaware myself, but crystals are deeply rooted in mysticism. Some people use them as healing tools, while others might use them to ward off evil spirits and bring good luck. They can even go as far as being used to contact spirits and angels. Whatever you are using them for, none of these practices line up with what the Bible says about this. God warns against such practices. Deuteronomy 18:9–12 says,

> *"When you enter the land the Lord your God is giving you,*
> *do not learn to imitate the detestable ways of the nations there.*
> *Let no one be found among you who sacrifices their son or daughter*
> *in the fire, who practices divination or sorcery, interprets omens,*
> *engages in witchcraft, or casts spells, or who is a medium or*
> *spiritist or who consults the dead. Anyone who does these things is*
> *detestable to the Lord; because of these same detestable practices,*
> *the Lord your God will drive out those nations before you."*

What is being described here are the practices of the occult. The more modern-day practices of this are the use of crystals, fortune tellers, magic, and burning sage to ward off bad energy.

You might say, well what's wrong with using crystals and sage? Sage purifies the air, and crystals are just pretty rocks, so what's the big deal?

You see, just because it's trendy doesn't mean it's okay. When you assign supernatural powers to anything, you downplay God's power. My owning a crystal will not guarantee me prosperity, peace, protection, or any of these types of things, so I advise you not to lean on such a thing to provide you with what only God can. All blood-washed, born-again Christians have access to a spiritual inheritance in Christ and the Holy Spirit. Anyone who is encouraging others to engage in New Age practices, like crystals, mediums, fortune tellers, or anything similar, is a part of the problem. You're sending confusing signals to a generation who are already growing up confused. If you are searching for a mentor or coach, and they are engaging in such practices, then keep looking. Anyone who claims to be godly should not be engaging in or promoting such things.

Remember, we are stewards, and at the end of the day, this is God's stuff we're managing, not our own. We must keep in mind that He is the one we report to and we should be careful not to engage in anything that undermines His power.

We must make sure we guard God's Kingdom by opposing New Age principles and standing firm in our faith. I understand the need to embrace trends,
some of them can be very powerful and advantageous in stewardship if they are
the right trends. However, if they are the wrong trends, it won't make God (our
manager) too happy. Ezekiel 13:18, 20–21 states it directly,

> *"Woe to the women who sew magic charms on all their wrists and*
> *make veils of various lengths for their heads in order to ensnare people.*
> *Will you ensnare the lives of my people but preserve your own? I am*
> *against your magic charms with which you ensnare people like birds,*
> *and I will tear them from your arms; I will set free the people that*
> *you ensnare like birds. I will tear off your veils and save my people*
> *from your hands, and they will no longer fall prey to your power."*

Yes, this is from the Old Testament, but God's disgust with occult practices
has not changed since then. He wasn't feeling them then, and He is not feeling
them now. God is not going to be okay with you engaging in and promoting
things He is disgusted with, especially if you're using them as your source of
power or to make money or lead others astray. This includes using crystals. All
these New Age products are just a glossier, more attractive version of the occult
packaged in sparkly pretty pinks and shiny crystals, which is why it mainly
draws the attention of women.

The thing that's scary about all this is that some women report receiving
some kind of power and change in circumstances in these practices. Please
understand the power is not coming from God because you are not operating
under His authority with these practices. You need to be very careful with this.
The devil is very crafty. When you engage in these practices, you will eventually
build systems based on New Age principles and birth businesses with founda-
tions based on these ungodly principles, and this is not God-honoring.

You think you are breaking generational curses, but you would actually
be building new ones. Ultimately, if you engage in these kinds of practices, you
end up corrupting the purpose God ordained for you. What's happening with
all this is the birth of a whole new generation that is not properly equipped
spiritually and terribly misinformed. The enemy is loving this New Age stuff
because it presents a warped view of Christianity. If we're misinformed from
the beginning, we are making his job a whole lot easier, and when that happens,
he stops bothering us. I mean, why would he need to? He has us right where
he would want us anyway. There's a saying that goes, "If the devil ain't messing
with you, you've already been defeated."

We are addicted to wanting to have as much control of the outcome as
possible, so we follow whatever trend that appears to be working to accomplish

If you engage in New Age practices, you end up corrupting the purpose God ordained for you.

that—crystals, charms, tarot cards, burning sage, whatever it may be. These trends have entered the mainstream, but more specifically, they have made the biggest impact on women's empowerment, which has built its foundation on New Age ideals. As women of God, you must remember where your source of power comes from. The minute something or someone else becomes your power source other than God, you remove yourself from His covenant, and that's not going to work out to your benefit. People are counting on you to use your gift appropriately. You never know whose life you are going to change.

The Church

The Church has an enormous responsibility in ensuring that people aren't misled. If there is any place that a Christian should be able to rely on for sound advice, it should be the local church. Some of the best business advice I've ever gotten has been from my pastor, whether it was from his sermons, Bible study, or internal counseling. It has always been sound, consistent, and reasonable. If you consider yourself to be a Christian and take your relationship with God seriously, then going to church shouldn't be optional. And now, since most things have been virtualized due to the pandemic, we really don't have an excuse. The issue these days is a lot of people think that they've outgrown the church. This is especially the case with Millennials, who look at the church as old and outdated. It's easy to get caught up in New Age ideas if you are not connected to a church.

This, of course, does not mean that everyone outside the church is into New Age practices, but it's easy to get sucked into it if you are not connected to a church where you are getting spiritually fed. Seeking guidance from your pastor, ministers, and other members can be very resourceful for you as a Christian entrepreneur or a professional. If you don't have a church home, not only are you missing out on a ministry but a whole support system.

Like I said before, the enemy is out to get you, so you want a support system, the *right* support system, behind you. Now, I'll be the first to tell you that the church needs some work when it comes to keeping up with the times. A lot of churches are not set up properly to provide the foundation that we Christian entrepreneurs need. However, when it comes to spiritual guidance, most churches are equipped, so get all you can from this beautiful resource.

Church is not all about being told how to live your life and what's right and wrong. People seem to think that's what the church is all about, but it's not. There have been plenty of times I've gotten very sound advice, advice that I've applied to build my brand and business. I understand the Church needs some work with being more innovative and open-minded, but it's one of the best resources to help ensure you are building on the right foundation. Think of it as going to school; most of us wouldn't be anywhere without an education.

You're probably thinking, "Well, the Church does have a reputation for being judgmental and old school," but this is not true for all churches, so I advise you not to dismiss all of them. Don't let the world cloud your judgment about the church. The church is a community waiting to support you. You just need to let your guard down and find one that suits you. I grew up Baptist, and I'm now a member of a church that happens to be Pentecostal. I ended up there through a referral from a friend. It had nothing to do with a preference on denomination; it just happened to be where I am getting fed spiritually.

My church is a bit more formal, but the fruit I was and still am getting from there is very ripe. I've met some very intelligent and resourceful people from just striking up a conversation. Some connections came from going to Bible study, while others came from other church events or simply fellowshipping and having conversations. All this networking is done free of charge. This is the only place where I can learn about salvation, theology, personal development, and steward-ship all in one place. What I'm trying to get at is for you not to completely dismiss the church, and if you do have a church home, then I would recommend getting more involved. The church isn't always included in the world of personal and professional development, but it can be with some improvements—a topic I will discuss later in this book. *The church is a network, a community, a family, an asset that shouldn't be excluded.*

When it comes to getting advice, the biggest takeaway I can give you is practicing discernment. No matter what resource you use, be sure to take note of the details because the details do matter. One small misuse of detail could throw your whole journey off course. A person who posts godly encouragement, and in the next breath starts promoting New Age principles, should raise a red flag. Would it be a good idea to hire this person to coach you? I would advise against including someone like that in your journey. Coaching and counseling are personal, so be mindful of whom you let into your personal space.

Beloved, I hope you understand what I am trying to convey to you. Not trying to tell you that you should only get advice from believers, no; I am just exposing you to truths that are not easily visible. This way, you will be able to make better decisions. Ask God to help you build discernment, and you will be able to better determine good advice from not just bad advice but *almost* good advice so you can get the best advice. Then, it will surely become much clearer the way you should go.

PART TWO

Build

<small>To develop according to a systematic plan,
by a definite process, or on a particular base.[11]</small>

4

The Process of Elimination

"Everybody cannot go where God is taking you."

E liminate defined is *"to remove or get rid of, especially as being in some way undesirable."* Or *"to omit, especially as being unimportant or irrelevant; leave out:"*[12] To thrive in your business and your calling, eliminate everything and everyone that do not add value or isn't part of the process. Eliminating people is often the hardest part because it also involves cutting people who do not serve you well. It's hard cutting out things that make you feel good or comfortable, things that make you feel accepted. Perhaps the hardest of all is cutting people out whom you love and respect. But everybody can't be a part of the equation, so they must be left out of it. What do you think your experience would be like letting everybody in especially when they don't add to the equation? Everybody who makes you feel good doesn't always add value, and everyone won't make the cut; *that's just the way it is.*

This chapter will cover everything you will need to exclude or eliminate from your life for you to thrive in whatever your calling is. Sometimes you need to make room, so you can have the clarity you need to see where God is taking you. You may need to let go of opportunities that don't align with your beliefs or people who bring you down or work against you. You may also need to take inventory of your social media, expenses, and even of yourself. We may even find ourselves missing out on valuable experiences, like trips, events, or anything that would make us experience FOMO (fear of missing out), and sometimes, it's for our own good. It's important you have a vacancy in your life so that God has room to develop you. God wants to help you develop your gifts. He does not want any talent left behind.

Eliminating People

My dear, not everybody is for you. Your gift is special, one of a kind—priceless, and it needs to be protected. Therefore, you can't work with just anybody because everybody is not suited to be involved in your development process. Some people used to be in my life that I could never be cool with again. Not that they did anything wrong, but they were friends with an older version of me. The old Maria was wild. I was a free spirit, a big-time smoker and drinker, and not many weekends went by where I wasn't turning up in a club somewhere. My actions may not seem like much to some but try telling that to God. I tried, and He didn't want to hear it. The new Maria is different, and when God changes your heart, the new you will be different too. Unfortunately, everybody is not going to accept the new you, and you must learn to be okay with that. You have to learn to be okay with people excluding you too.

When you commit your life to the Lord, He makes you into a new creature. Ephesians 4:22–24 (ESV) says to "put off your old self, which belongs to your former manner of life and is corrupt through deceitful desires, and to be renewed in the spirit of your minds, and to put on the new self, created after the likeness of God in true righteousness and holiness."

You see, to truly become whom you're supposed to be, there is a spiritual transformation you must go through first. "To put off your old self, which belongs to your former manner of life" means to turn from your old ways and eliminate the things that could potentially keep you from properly walking in your purpose.

That means you can't work with everybody either. You might admire a particular person, but they may not be right for you. There are people I admired but now admire from afar. It was hard unenrolling from their courses and mentorship programs, but they no longer served me. I'm sorry, but when God is involved, *some people gotta go.* I showed you in the previous chapter how to filter these people out through discernment, which will help you determine whom you can and can't work with. I love helping people tell their stories. Storytelling is one of my strongest suits as a writer and as someone who works in the marketing field, but let me tell you, everyone's story is not meant for me to

*To truly become whom you're supposed to be, there is
a spiritual transformation you must go through first.*

tell. If what you're trying to market goes against my Kingdom values, then sorry, but I can't help you with that. As Christians, we need to make that clear from the beginning. I'm not the one, no matter how much you pay me. You cannot work with everybody, and everybody can't work with you, period.

Sometimes, we have to make the unfortunate decision to end relationships that no longer serve us. I've had to do the same. Just like you can't work with everybody, the same applies to personal relationships–everybody can't come. It will be hard for you to thrive if you bring everybody into your space. That's why it's always crowded at the bottom, and, unfortunately, thins out at the top. One thing is for sure, though, if you are being a good steward, people will begin to exclude themselves. This includes friends, family, or associates you trust. They will distance themselves when they see you are taking your relationship with the Lord seriously. A lot is revealed in this process. It's both painful and enlightening.

Eliminating Friendships

Our friends are not in our lives by happenstance; they were meant to be there, whether for a short time or a lifetime. I am blessed to have solid friendships and a strong support system; it does make a difference. However, there are times when I've had to choose between purpose and friendship. Have you ever wondered why millionaires and successful people tend to not have a lot of friends? When you get to a certain point in your journey, your friends do tend to take a backseat. This is not always intentional, but it happens. Unless they add value or are on the same journey as you are, they usually get left behind.

During this period of growth, your friends may start to look different, not in a bad way, just different. You may not do the same things or be able to relate the same anymore. This is where the process of elimination begins. You either remain friends, or you don't; they either stick around and encourage you, or they get impatient and the friendship fades. You might get impatient with them as well. You need friends who can grow with you and even more, so understand that this journey you're on is not easy. You may not always be able to hang out, and your friends need to understand that you might be going through a lot. "She is always busy, but I'm happy she is pursuing her goals. It must be hard, so I'm gonna support her," is what they should be thinking. I'm blessed to have friends who when I'm MIA (missing in action), know, "Oh, she must be working on something." They don't just assume the worst and cancel me! If you have friends who automatically jump to the cancel conclusions or can't offer encouragement, then it may be time for you to reevaluate your circle.

The more successful you become, the more clear it will become who your real friends are. Your circle will get smaller.

You cannot please everybody, and I've never known a time where that was ever acceptable. Even Jesus didn't please everybody. He stuck with His Father's plan, and that's what you should be focused on as well. Your real friends will stick around; they might even be a part of your plan one day. You would know who your real friends are because you wouldn't have to keep explaining yourself to them. They'll just know and will be rooting for you. The more successful you become, the more clear it will become who your real friends are. Your circle will get smaller. It's just the cost of being successful.

Sometimes, the more-the-merrier idea doesn't always fit. Quality isn't in the number of people; it's in the type of people you associate with. Quality is the way they make you feel. When measuring success, the whole quality-over-quantity thing is true. For example, look at how most luxury brands run their companies. They only produce so many products at once, as opposed to a cheaper brand that puts out three times as much but the quality is mediocre. Or a restaurant with a one-page menu versus one with a ten-page menu, think a small high-end steakhouse versus a large restaurant chain. Which one would have the best food? The same thing applies with friends and associates; the more people in your circle, the more quantity will supersede quality. It's hard to create genuine relationships with people when you have too many people around you because you run the risk of spreading yourself too thin. My circle has gone up and down over the years and is now at a size I'm comfortable with. I love my circle being small; I've learned to accept it. Do you want to be successful? Then your circle is going to get smaller too, so learn to accept it.

For me, where I am with this season in my life, I don't need people in my life who don't add value, and neither do you. Everybody is not going to stick around; that is a part of growth. Romans 8:28 (KJV) says, "And we know that all things work together for good to them that love God, to them who are the called according to his purpose." All things are working for your good, so continue to work on what supports the bigger picture, and don't worry about who sticks around and who doesn't.

Excluding Opportunities

Have you ever refused to work on a project or decline an opportunity? I have, and it was not easy. I've turned down job opportunities that offered very competitive pay and benefits. I tried to make every excuse about why it was a great opportunity, but my spirit just wouldn't let me take it. The company I had to turn down had strong New Age values that I'm sure would have been the foundation of the campaigns I would have been hired to run. Some industries are harder than others, like acting, for instance. To my actors and actresses, I don't know how you do it. As a Christian, I would imagine it must be hard as heck to work in this field because you have to be super picky. Are you sure you want to take that part? If there's a risqué scene, would you do it? Would the money be worth your reputation as a saint?

Remember, there are some things worth more than money, your reputation is one of them. You need to be clear about where you stand because, eventually, the world is going to see the fruit you produce. When you accept a position that goes against your beliefs, keep in mind that no one knows the day or the hour when Christ will return. No one likes to hear that, but it's true. I have to remind myself that as well because it's so easy to lose your way. This is especially hard if you operate in front-facing roles, like acting, modeling, or any career where you

*'You need to be clear about ᷄where you
stand in your faith ᷄because the world is
going to see the fruit you produce.*

are front and center. I'm going to say a special prayer for Christians who operate
in these kinds of careers!

No matter what, don't let anyone talk you into compromising. Remember,
we are stewards first, and if anyone you are working with isn't cool with that,
then the relationship is not meant to be. I think statements like that scare people
because relationships are so important. Don't worry, as I said before, stick to
God's plan, and He will place the right people in your life. Excluding people,
places, and things from your life comes with the territory; just like holidays,
some people are seasonal. Sometimes seasons last for just a few months or
sometimes a few years. Just keep looking at the bright side—you are going to
inherit so much more if you continue to do what's right for the Kingdom. Saying
no can be the beginning of so many yesses.

FOMO

There are times when people may exclude you from some things. This is another
part of this journey that doesn't feel good but is necessary. It might not always
happen on purpose but it happens. You might not get the invite to the party
because people may assume you're too busy. We've all experienced this; I am
experiencing it in real-time. I have always been very driven, wanting something
better, newer, and many of my friends know that, so I wouldn't always get an
invite. In addition to that, I am married; we've been together for over seventeen
years and married for over five years, so I am used to people making assumptions about my availability. The more you grow, the more assumptions people
will start to make; the more focused you become, the fewer people will reach

out. This is where FOMO will start to set in. FOMO is the fear of missing out—that fear that others are having fun without you, or you're missing out on something great.

If you've ever felt this, it can get depressing, trust me I know. While living out of the country for over five years, I felt the sting of FOMO daily. It was rough, and I even went through a depressing period because of it. Whether it was a personal FOMO, seeing pictures of my friends at parties I couldn't attend, or FOMO over the historical events taking place in the States that I didn't have the privilege to be a part of — I'm still sad about missing all the 2020 protests; I truly wanted to be a part of that. What has helped me was realizing how impactful my purpose will be and how I will help so many people. For me, that is better and much more important than being a part of everything else. That is how I am able to get past my FOMO.

I've also embraced my creative side more. I was writing every day: blogs, poetry, writing prompts, short stories, anything I could do to keep me enlightened and creative. I employ you to do this as well. Dive into your creativity, and I promise you, the FOMO will fade. The funny thing is when I would be invited out, there were times when I would turn it down and when I heard about it later, my friends would tell me, "Girl, you didn't miss a thing." Facts, because it was no different from any other time we've gone out. You have to get better at delaying gratification if you want to be successful. You have to ask yourself, *What am I missing that I haven't already experienced?* I've come to realize that sometimes being overlooked could work to your advantage. The things coming your way will be better than anything you were excluded from if you continue to do the work.

Social Media

Social media is a necessary evil. Sometimes we hate it, and sometimes we love it. If you are an entrepreneur or trying to start a brand or business, then social media will be your best friend. Honestly, you won't be able to escape it. Instagram is still the most dominant and TikTok is quickly creeping up to take its place. If you have quality followers, you'll reap the benefits. The same can be said if you are following quality people, people who add value. However, there's another side to social media that can become distracting if you are not managing it correctly. For example, you don't need to follow 5,000 people! You are just asking for distractions. It wouldn't hurt to clean out your social media every now and then. I try to do a monthly clean out of my Instagram, and while doing that, I notice that most of the people I was following are all doing the same thing, just labeling their profiles differently. *It just isn't necessary for me to follow ten different coaches.* I would recommend you eliminate what's not adding value and curate your feed in a way so it helps you and doesn't distract you. You want to be able to use Instagram as a tool to stay up on trends and connect with your audience— having a feed full of people who don't add value will only distract from that. Unfollowing is part of the process. People expect it anyway.

One last thing you may want to consider is cutting social media altogether. *You said to do what?* Yes, sometimes it's necessary. The longest I went without social media was a week, and let me tell you, the mental clarity I had after that was incredible. Sometimes you need to give it a break so you can take a step back and strategize. Use it, but don't get consumed by it.

EXPENSES AND SERVICES

When it comes to the process of elimination, expenses certainly come to mind. If there is ever an area where we needed help managing, it would be our expenses. You don't need twenty different tools for your business. I know it's easy to get caught up in making your business look pretty, spending money on fancy branding and trendy marketing tools, but don't become a business tool junkie. Some things aren't necessary. Maybe you don't need a bunch of fancy business cards and fancy stationery because all these shiny add-ons do add up. Maybe consider the fancy stuff later when you are making enough to where you still have money left over after you cover expenses. Learn what's best for you and your business first before spending tons of money. For instance, if you regularly do webinars and video coaching, then it may be advantageous for you to look into purchasing a Zoom plan or some other video conferencing software instead of using the free version. The free version could work for you, but as always, everything depends on business needs.

When you are in the beginning stages of your business, you are likely to explore more, so you're more likely to make the most mistakes, and that's okay. This is one reason why it may be beneficial to hire a coach or take a course to help steer you in the right direction. It may not be a bad idea to fit these types of things into your budget. The bottom line is that you want to make sure you spend money on the right resources that best suit your business from the beginning. You want to do this for your personal development as well.

I would even consider the people around you—what do your friends do for a living? Do they have any skillsets that could help cut down your expenses? Can you trade services, you do something for them in return for them doing something for you? You could save a ton of money this way and cancel out having to purchase a bunch of do-it-yourself marketing tools. Figuring out what matters the most is a process, so try to figure out as much as you can from the beginning. If you have people in your circle that can help, that's even better. I would take advantage of any of the talents and gifts anyone can offer you.

Eliminating Doubt

This is the one. Doubt should be one of the first things to eliminate from your life. Doubt is a dream-killer; believe me, I know. I used to have a real problem with it. I would secure a job, then doubt if I could do it. I doubted if I could do a good job and then I'd actually do a good job, but then I'd doubt if I could do it again. Once I get over one doubt another would replace it, and that's no way to live. You can't ask God for something and then doubt it in the next breath. When they say faith without works is dead, that's true, but you can't do the work and doubt yourself at the same time. Just look at all God has done for you so far! If you are alive right now, then God has done something for you at some point. All doubt does is slow down the process. Look at what James 1:6 (KJV) says, "But let him ask in faith, with no doubting, for the one who doubts is like a wave of the sea that is driven and tossed by the wind."

Doubt just throws you back and forth, never getting you anywhere. Don't be tossed by the wind, saints. If God has something for you, it's already there, but you just have to get to it. If you believe you won't get it, then you won't — it's as simple as that. The doubt and the mental clutter have to go, or it will handicap you if it doesn't. One of my favorite quotes that sums up doubt is a quote by Henry Ford, "Whether you think you can, or you think you can't – you're right."[13]

You don't need a lot of people in your life to make things happen. Likewise, you don't need a lot of tools to make things work. Most of the time, less is more. Sometimes, there needs to be a vacancy in your life so you can hear God's voice. This means getting rid of people, places, and things. I could recall a time in my life when I went on a cleaning spree. I deleted people from my phone, my social media, and my life. I would say to you to do the same thing—clean up and clean out! At one point, I even went as far as to delete my Instagram account and start over.

Sometimes you must destroy to rebuild because you can't build on a mess.

Sometimes you must destroy to rebuild because you can't build on a mess. Perhaps the biggest clean-out of all will be the mental clean-out. For me, it was the deliverance from doubt. You wouldn't believe the peace of mind I had. Once you get rid of the physical and mental clutter, you will have more room to include the things that add to your life and your purpose. It's hard to function in a cluttered space. I don't know how anyone could be successful that way.

Cleaning out the mental and physical clutter will allow you to see what's necessary and what isn't. Some things you need, some things you don't; some people you need, some people you don't. With the process of elimination, you decide who and what adds to your life and make decisions based on that. God doesn't want us to have less, He just wants us to have more room for the good stuff.

5

Follow-Unfollow

Unfollowing is business as usual, so go ahead, unfollow me. It's nothing new. People are going to unfollow you anyway no matter who you are. You cannot let that change how you build your business or let the way people feel about you disrupt your flow. It's so easy to do away with people these days, especially with foolish trends like cancel culture where just one off-color comment can get you canceled. *Such different times we're living in, right?* With a click of a button, they will never see you in their feed again, and you have to be okay with that. You have to be okay with being canceled by people around you too. The important thing is to have the right followers who look to you to help them in some way, whether it's your product, skill, or godly encouragement, and to follow those who benefit you in the same ways.

We are living in times where opinions matter more than ever before. We care so much about what people think that we will develop our business models just to support their feelings. Getting more likes and followers don't guarantee success. Most people tend to follow what's trendy and cling to what makes them feel good, which is why more followers don't mean more profits. Why do you think celebrities, Instagram models, and comedians typically have more followers than a business coach or entrepreneur? It's an escape for most people. People like to laugh and look at eye candy, that's just the way it is. Now, let's take a look at what does and doesn't matter, and what your main focus should be when it comes to creating content to get the right followers.

Numbers Don't Always Matter

When it comes to social media, numbers don't always matter, but influence does. Follower count is very misleading because you don't necessarily know the reason someone is following you. It can be automation (meaning bots, yeah, people still use these), you're attractive, their friend is following you, or they like your product or what you have to say. They may be following you because you might be a potential customer for them. You could be *their* target market. Honestly, you won't know why they're following you until you brand yourself correctly. Only then will you be able to really see God's plan for you come to fruition. Not branding correctly could interfere with His plan and slow things down for you. As the saying goes, delayed doesn't mean denied, but do you really want to be delayed any further? You can do what's required to see who's really for you and get the right people on your side so that you don't waste time. Your content helps develop your brand identity and gives people an idea of the type of person you are. If you are a female entrepreneur whose goal is to attract other millennial female entrepreneurs, but you attract mostly men, well then, something is not right there.

So, how do you properly develop your brand identity? Create content that is relevant to your brand or business that speaks to your target market. Your content will be your catalyst for the kind of audience you attract. For example, take the two magazine giants "Cosmopolitan" and "Black Enterprise." These are two totally different magazine brands that have completely different audiences because of the content they create.

That was an easy one, so let's look at something less obvious. What if you were an aspiring coach whose target market is female entrepreneurs in the beauty and wellness space, particularly estheticians and massage therapists, but all you are attracting are hairstylists? It's great they are following you, but they are not your target market. You may even land one of them as a client but still, your expertise is not set up to properly serve them. It's set up to help women in specific areas in the wellness space. It's possible that your branding and profile information is too generic. Instead of saying something like, "I help female entre-preneurs grow their brands in the beauty and wellness industry," it should say something like, "I help estheticians and massage therapists build their personal brand to land reoccurring clients." It's very specific, to the point, and solves a problem right in the description. The formula looks like this:

> *"I help this specific group of people build this specific*
> *thing to achieve these specific results."*

'Your content helps develop your 'brand identity' and gives people an idea of the type of person you are.

When you get specific, it eliminates any confusion about whom you serve or the results you plan to get for them. Maybe you're attracting too many ghost followers, that is, people who don't click like or comment on anything. This could mean you need to make your content more interesting. Start doing videos and add more CTA's to your posts. A good CTA asks your followers questions or invites them to check out some of your services, more on this detail later in the chapter on marketing. All this to say, numbers are one thing but organic followers are the real thing. Once you start branding yourself the right way, you'll see your numbers go up and down. But, not to worry, this up and down process must happen to filter out the invaluable people—it's necessary for growth. With that, you'll be able to quickly tell the real from the fake because the real people will stick around and actually engage with your CTA.

REBRANDING FOR GOD

If you are ready to take the call God has on your life seriously, then you might be in a position where you need to consider rebranding, and with rebranding comes a loss of support, or in the case of social media loss of followers. I was reading an article on Christianpost.com about former Victoria's Secret-model-turned-Christian-activist Nicole Weider, who walked away from a very lucrative modeling career to follow Jesus. This is a woman who has completely changed her life for God. The article quoted her saying, "I realized that being a model was truly not what it was cracked up to be. I felt degraded, that I was never 'perfect' enough, and being judged only on my appearance was hurting my self-esteem. I realized I wanted more for my life. I rediscovered my faith that I

Stay consistent with the call God has on your life, and the right people will come around and stick with you.

had as a little girl, and it changed my life because I was passionate about using my gifts for God instead of the empty modeling industry."[14] And she did it, too! She rebranded herself for God. Can you imagine all of the people she probably lost because of this decision? Not just followers on social media but in her life, all because of this bold choice. Talk about trimming the fat! Giving up all that money and popularity for God—do you think it was worth it?

Of course! God is always worth it.

People always tend to act funny when you take this route, so be ready for that. Nicole is now producing faith-based films and completely changed her branding to suit God's calling. She even dresses differently and is still stylish and beautiful. She is stunning, actually. I'm sure she is a lot happier and healthier too, at least she seems to be from what I can see on social media. She has a husband and recently had a baby. I follow her on Instagram; she's a doll! I'm sure, without a doubt, God has blessed her beyond anything the modeling industry could offer. Stay consistent with the call God has on your life, and the right people will come around and stick with you.

Stories like hers are so inspiring that it makes me want to step up my game in my own rebranding process. I've rebranded a number of times—renaming my website, starting a new Instagram, and finally creating a TikTok page. What makes it so difficult is that you cannot hide while doing it. Everybody is going to see the changes you make. Changing your brand name? People are going to notice. Updating your brand colors? People are going to notice, but guess what? This is the way business works so who cares what people think?

Physically rebranding is not as hard as you think. Things like changing your logo, brand colors, and changing your Instagram name are the easy parts; the hard part is accepting the fact that some people will not like the new you. I'm sure Nicole figured that out, and you will too.

Through my curiosity about Ms. Weider's transition, I was surprised to find that there are a lot of models who have made that same transition to Christ. One even mentioned how shortly after a fashion show she dropped to her knees in prayer because it had gotten that bad. Is having a lot of followers and people staring at your most-likely photoshopped pictures or one-minute videos worth this kind of pain? I think more women are getting to the point where they don't believe the pain is worth it. Don't worry about people unfollowing you or not supporting you because there's a bigger support system waiting for you! You will know who supports you because they'll stick around. Look at the big picture. There are going to be people cheering you on who, like me, you wouldn't even expect! It's going to be just fine!

Unfollow Them

You like her brand and love her style and even purchased some of the cute merch she sells. She's adored by everyone, and you've been following her for a while, but something is off about her. As I've mentioned, I've had to unfollow people I adored because they started promoting things that did not align with my beliefs. To me, their brand was tainted and no longer resonated with me. I have to admit, I missed seeing their pretty pictures in my feed, but the real truth about the person behind the brand outweighed what they were posting. We have to come to the conclusion that no matter how trendy something is, some things just gotta go.

Try auditing the actions of the influencers you follow before you go too deep with them. What are they posting? Does their profile say one thing, but they do another? Are they engaged with their audience enough? Do they respond to their comments? These are the things you should be looking at to determine whether or not you should continue following them. This is especially important if you're looking for a coach or mentor.

If you are serious about your calling, unfollow people who talk about God but promote things contradictory to His nature. I swear this is what bothers me the most. There are just too many influencers to mention who do this. I pray for them, but they won't get my time, attention, or money. As I stated in the previous chapter, sometimes you need to do a digital detox and get rid of people anyway. Some people have no place in your feed no matter how positive they might appear. So go ahead—unfollow them; they won't miss you anyway.

Chances are they got way too many people following them to notice and too many people validating them to care. They're just going to keep doing what they think is right.

It does make me think, though. I wonder how God really feels about social media? It can be a great tool when used correctly, but if we're not careful, it can be the perfect tool for the enemy. So, my sister, beware who you are opening the door to. One of my favorite verses is 1 John 4:1 (KJV), "Beloved, believe not every spirit, but try the spirits whether they are of God: because many false prophets are gone out into the world."

This verse talks about discernment, something we all need to exercise more in our lives and businesses. I can't tell you how many times I've subconsciously used sketchy ideas in my own marketing that I wouldn't have had I not exposed myself to them. I stopped following a lot of people after I realized the role the subconscious plays in storing content. It will quietly lead you to places you shouldn't go. *How sneaky is that?* You should be aware that this is one of the enemy's favorite tricks.

I've unfollowed a lot of people these days. I'm sad I had to because they really did add to my life in some ways. But they got too caught up in the New Age trap. It's a shame because these are bright and intelligent women who have a lot to offer but started promoting ideas that were tainted with New Age beliefs. There is a lot of this going on, especially with wellness influencers who give really helpful information but wrap it in spiritual mysticism.

Meditation, mindfulness, and going vegan are all good stuff, but they have become heavily associated with New Age ideals: Chakras, crystals, connecting with the universe (not God). These are also the types of posts that get high engagement, which is proof that these worldly ideas are spreading. As a steward of God, while you are building your business, I want you to be aware of the details because the details do make a difference. If the details are not taken seriously, they will spread into something more serious. Anything that is sending mixed messages is like dumping salt over a bowl of fresh fruit. Is it helping or harming? It can't be both.

As hard as this might be, you will have to start the unfollowing process. Whether they unfollow you or you unfollow them, unfollowing is a part of growth. There's a saying that goes, "You must destroy in order to rebuild." Unfollow anybody who gets in your way, clouding the Kingdom agenda. You

Some people have no place in your feed no matter how positive they might appear. So go ahead—unfollow them.

don't have to necessarily stop using their services if they are good at what they do, you just don't need them in your personal space.

Use social media as a tool to build, promote, and grow your business, but don't allow it to lead you to consume the wrong content. You could end up building your business or brand on some principle that is not aligned with God and you won't even know it. Additionally, you don't need to follow thousands of people to find inspiration or the help you need. I've been down that road, and a very convincing road it was. Thank God my discernment is getting better. Had it not, I would have kept getting sucked into the social media rabbit hole. So yes, my love, unfollow anyone who does not add value to what you are building. It's okay if they unfollow you too; it may be proof that you are moving in the right direction, so let them. Whatever the reason, unfollowing is a part of growth.

6

Competition

Competition.

You can either run away from it, with it or against it. There is always going to be someone doing better than you but you don't know what it took for them to get where they are now. A rule of thumb I live by is to never compare your beginning to someone else's ending. And just in case no one told you, *you're already a winner anyway.*

Imagine running a race where each person who crossed the finish line all got first place trophies and cash prizes. Each trophy looked different, but they were all first-place trophies personalized with the winner's name engraved on them. Everybody won; they just had to make it to the finish line. The only rule was that they had to actually *run* the race.

The race I want to discuss is the race of success. Everybody runs this race differently, so you want to make sure your running shoes fit. Competition is inevitable, but everybody is not running with the same shoes on. For example, a person living in California who is trying to build a fashion brand is going to have a different process than someone trying to do the same thing in Cleveland. The aspiring fashion designer in Cleveland would quite possibly have to move to California or a big city like New York to be in close proximity to the heavy hitters in that industry. Therefore, they may have an extra step in their process versus someone already living in these places. That doesn't mean they won't be successful; it also doesn't mean they can't be a successful designer if they choose to stay in Cleveland. They just will have some extra steps, and that's totally fine.

I've known people who relocated and started businesses and ended up surpassing their peers living in the places they have relocated to. You would think that the people living there would surpass them but that's not always the

Never compare your beginning to someone else's ending.

case. Nothing is supposed to be fair. I mean nothing ever will be, so don't get caught up in competition. God has everyone in different positions and circumstances for a reason, so your winning formula is going to be different. Wear the shoes that fit you and focus on what you need to do to get there.

"There is no competition. I am my own competition." That's what I always tell myself, and it applies to you as well. No one can compete because we are all made by glorious hands, and those hands didn't make any mistakes. God made us all with unique qualities, and even though we may have some of the same talents and abilities, we operate in them differently. So just be yourself. I know it's something we've all heard before but the reason we keep hearing it is that it's true. Allowing God to shape you into a better version of yourself is the blueprint. It has taken longer than it needed for me to realize this. I used to think that I had to follow a specific process or someone else's formula for success, and I couldn't have been more wrong. I've lost count of how many webinars I've joined, courses I've purchased, and marketing videos I've watched. One formula I followed was that you can't make your posts too personal if you want to grow your business. I've heard this from very popular influencers, and it's neither right nor wrong, in my opinion. It all depends on the business or brand you are building. For me, I have to get personal; that seems to be the only thing that works for me.

I believe to be successful, there must be a delicate balance of both personal and professional. We have to be vulnerable enough, giving our audience a chance to get to know us, while at the same time remaining professional. People love it when you can still be you and professional at the same time. I'll tell you, out of all the strategies I've tried, the one that has worked for me the most was just being myself. I found that the personal posts got more followers (quality followers). I've tried every strategy you can imagine, posting at a specific time a day, running Facebook Ads, and spending more time than I needed creating graphics. These strategies worked somewhat, but things didn't really start taking off for me until I started being more vulnerable—until I started letting people in more. Let me encourage you to be yourself and stay genuine, while at the same time consistently perfecting your craft. I think you'll see things work out in your favor.

Look to Collaboration

Sometimes, I think we should work together more. I think there are too many people out there doing the same thing but with different titles. When I was looking for a coach, I got to a point where when it came time to choose one, I had to narrow it down from twenty people to fifteen to ten, then finally narrowed it down to five coaches. If coaching is your calling, then go for it. Who am I to tell you what you should do? After all, it is your legacy, not mine. I just think that certain industries are oversaturated. I've always wanted to start my own marketing agency, but there are just so many out there. For a while, I ended up shifting my focus to collaborating instead. It may sound like I'm giving up, but I'm just choosing to extend my services to people who might need them by working alongside them instead of competing against them. Also, there is enough room for all of us. Ask yourself, is there someone who would be more beneficial for me to collaborate with than to compete with? As the saying goes, if you can't beat 'em, join 'em. Together, you and your collaboration partners could become a powerhouse.

Allowing God to shape you into a better version of yourself is the blueprint.

❖

One example is a very dear friend of mine, who is also a writer. She was thinking of starting her own freelance writing agency. I got a little worried because, without a doubt, she is a fantastic writer, probably better than me. *This girl is gonna be tough competition,* I thought. Instead, she asked me if I could add her services to my website. She needed a space to expand her freelance services, so she asked me to help her versus creating a whole website for herself.

So, when she asked me to join *with her,* I was like, "Of course!" You see, we are all entrepreneurs to some degree and have a natural ability to want to create something and call it our own. But even as entrepreneurs, there are times when we should consider partnering up. If someone is doing the same thing you are doing but has something you can use, then consider collaborating instead of competing. Collaboration is one of the best ways to build your business, so use it as a tool to grow and nurture business relationships as well. You don't always have to be the competition; instead, be the solution. The big thing to remember is there is enough space for everybody.

COMPARISON

Comparing yourself to others doesn't solve or win you anything. It's unproductive and uses up energy that could be used to build something spectacular. Comparing is a waste of time for everyone because God has already laid out a plan for each and every one of us. We just have to have the courage to pursue it. Comparison is a funny thing. It's like you're trying to fit into someone else's standard, while at the same, they're trying to fit into what they think *your* standard is. I'm telling you, it's a fruitless cycle. To add to this cycle, when it comes to marketing entities, like social media, we are all competing with an invisible algorithm that doesn't even allow our content to be seen by everyone anyway. We are all fighting this battle to be the best of the best while there are systems working against all of us, isn't that something? So, when we compare, what does it really do? What can it do? Everyone has greatness in them that no one can duplicate, so when we compare, it just keeps us from finding out what that greatness is.

One exercise I've done in the past that has really worked is writing a letter to my younger self. My letter went something like this:

> *"I encourage you to embrace all the things that people think are weird about you and, most importantly, to remember who your Father is. Jeremiah 1:5 states, 'Before I formed you in the womb I knew you; Before you were born I sanctified you; I ordained you a prophet to the nations.' Keep this verse in mind whenever you start comparing yourself."*

Everyone has greatness in them
that no one can duplicate, so when we compare,
it just keeps us from finding out what that greatness is.

I don't know about you, but I want to find out who this person is before God formed me. *He says He knew me before I was even formed.* Wow, who am I? Who are you? If you continue to compare yourself to others, you will never find out.

The other side of comparison is that we are living in a time of great creativity, a time where there are plenty of seats at the table. There are so many opportunities to stand out. Let whatever light God has planted in you shine through, but you have to trust your light and you most certainly have to trust Him. Don't you know that you are fearfully and wonderfully made? Psalm 139:14 (KJV), says, "I will praise thee; for I am fearfully and wonderfully made: marvellous are thy works; and that my soul knoweth right well." When I look at this verse, the one thing that always sticks out to me is the "fearfully made" part. What does it mean to be fearfully and wonderfully made? Fearfully made means that whoever created such a thing is certainly someone not to be messed with. Whoever created us should be feared and worshipped! Imagine seeing something created with so much detail that it makes you wonder how in the world someone could do this. That is what you should think about when you start to compare. God constructed you with so much detail, character, and, most importantly, with so much love, that no matter how competitive things get, no one can compare to you.

Become Your Own Niche

Be yourself and stay consistent, and the rest will take care of itself. There are tons of examples of this on social media. For example, I follow a brand on social media that designs puzzles with images of children from diverse backgrounds and an illustrator who creates spiritually-inspired adult coloring books. These are very creative and distinct niches created solely from the person's talent more so than a strategy. You can also create a niche within a niche. Let's say you are a fashion designer, and you design clothes for adults and children. One way to create a niche within a niche is by designing matching outfits for moms and daughters, otherwise known as "mommy and me" and "dads and sons." You can post pictures on Instagram with both the dad and the son in the picture with the same outfit on to showcase how good the outfits look in either size. The dad may have on a fancy blazer, a trendy baseball cap, and nice slacks, and the son (maybe around kindergarten age) has on the same outfit. Mommy-and-me outfits are actually quite popular. Get creative and come up with a theme to separate yourself from other designers that are doing this. The point is, the more niche you are, the more likely people will remember you. God gave us all unique abilities, so let's capitalize on that. Someone can try to copy you, but the paste will never be the same, so enjoy winning in the lane you created!

What's Your Story?

Building your own niche is one thing, but telling your story is the real game-changer. Everybody has a story to tell, so tell yours! Your story is the one thing that no one can ever take from you because everybody's story is different. No one on this planet has the exact same story. Even if you grew up with someone in the same household, your stories will still be different. My own story of relocating to another country is unique in its own right, and that's only part of it. I'm sure you have something unique about you that makes you stand out too.

Speaking of standing out, I've got a story for you. Queens, New York, native, Marie Van Brittan Brown, invented the first home security system. Her desire to create such a system was influenced by the security risk her home faced in the neighborhood where she lived. Her original invention was a combination of peepholes, a camera, monitors, and a two-way microphone. The finishing touch was an alarm button that you could press to contact the police immediately. Later, to secure her efforts, Marie, along with her husband, Albert Brown, filed for a patent on August 1, 1966, and set the foundation for modern home security systems still in use today. So yes, the first home security system was invented by Marie Van Britton Brown, a black woman from Queens, New York. Marie's invention was birthed solely out of the desire to keep her and her family safe. Seems like a natural response to me; she just took it a step further. Today, small businesses, single-family homes, and multi-unit apartments around the world all have adopted Marie's technology. In addition to this huge accomplishment, she is also credited with the invention of the first closed-circuit television.[15]

You might say, "Well, I'm not an inventor," or "There's nothing *that* interesting about me"—just stop right there. First of all, everything God makes is interesting. Whether it's inventing the first home security system, like Marie Van Brittan Brown, or you're the first in your family to go to college, you are interesting either way. Let me encourage you to take some time and write down all your strengths, talents, and abilities to really take inventory of yourself. You would be surprised how seeing it all on paper makes you feel. I always recommend journaling as a great tool to use for your own self-esteem and self-discovery. When you write down your story, you can see for yourself, and say, "You know what? I'm a star!" This is how you begin to separate yourself from the competition; your story helps you create your own lane.

Brilliance

No matter who you are or where you come from, my dear, you are brilliant. I brought up the point of being fearfully and wonderfully made for a reason. Brilliant defined means, "striking, distinctive; distinguished by unusual mental keenness or alertness." Brilliant defined as a noun means "a gem (such as a diamond) cut in a particular form with numerous facets so as to have special brightness or brilliance."[16] God has planted a light inside you, me, all of us. Our God is brilliant, and His creation is brilliant, so that includes you, too. Let's look at some women with the most brilliant minds in history who have incredible stories to share.

Alice Augusta Ball

Born on July 24, 1892, in Seattle, Washington, Alice Augusta Ball was a black chemist who developed the first successful treatment for leprosy. She was also the very first black woman to graduate with an MS degree in chemistry from the College of Hawaii (now known as the University of Hawaii). Her method of treatment, known as the "Ball Method," was so successful that leprosy patients were discharged from hospitals around the world, including from Kalaupapa, an isolation facility on the north shore of Molokai, Hawaii, where thousands of leprosy patients died in years prior.[17]

Mae C. Jemison

Mae C. Jemison became the first black woman to be admitted into NASA's astronaut training program, and ultimately, the first black woman to explore space. Before she became an astronaut, she was a consistent honor student, a physician, and taught medical research before she fulfilled her iconic role as the first black woman astronaut. Mae has been inducted into the National Women's Hall of Fame, National Medical Association Hall of Fame, and Texas Science Hall of Fame, and has received numerous awards and recognitions to date. In addition to these achievements, she is also fluent in Russian, Japanese, and Swahili.[18]

Virginia Apgar

This brilliant and compassionate woman developed a process for the most fragile beginnings of life that we all should be thankful for, especially women. Virginia is the first woman to develop a standardize method in assessing the health of newborns. Her realization that the hospital systems had no standardized way to assess the health of newborns, along with her compassion for the health of newborns, and her distinguished background in anesthesiology, is what prompted this much-needed process. Her areas of assessment came to be known as the Apgar Score, and included the following: appearance, pulse, grimace, activity, and respiration. A vast amount of credit is due to Ms. Apgar as many newborn lives have likely been saved thanks to her method.[19]

Patricia Bath

Another brilliant mind, Patricia Bath, born November 4, 1942, in Harlem, was the first black woman, *respectfully the first black person,* to complete a residency in Ophthalmology, a branch of medicine and surgery that deals with the diagnosis and treatment of eye disorders, in 1973. She also became the first female faculty member in the Department of Ophthalmology at UCLA's Jules Stein Eye Institute and went on to help co-found the American Institute for the Prevention of Blindness in 1976. However, she didn't stop there. In 1981, Bath introduced to the world her most notable invention, the Laserphaco Probe, a device that created a less painful and more precise treatment of cataracts. She received a patent for the device in 1988, becoming the first black doctor ever to receive a patent for a medical purpose. She holds patents worldwide, including in Canada, Japan, and Europe. Perhaps the most astonishing part of her story was that with her invention, she was able to help restore the sight of people who had been blind for more than thirty years! Now if that's not what brilliance looks like, then I don't know what is. Her passion of restoring sight extended to North Africa while on a humanitarian mission, which, according to Bath, was her "best personal moment." On this mission, Bath restored the sight of a woman who had been blind for thirty years by using a process called kerato-prosthesi where an artificial cornea is implanted.[20] Can you believe it? Look at the things we are able to do!

There are so many more brilliant minds to mention, the list could go on forever. Do you think these people were worried about competition? I don't think they were. They simply saw a problem and were passionate enough about it to create a solution. Brilliant people nurture their God-given talents and abilities, and it works every time. You've probably heard the term, "They're in a league of their own." These are people who are not necessarily trying to create their own lane but their brilliance and passion create a lane for them. What I want you to understand is that we all have this level of capability to be as great as the most brilliant minds in history. What stands out most with brilliant people is that they are not just consistent, they take it a step further and devote their life to nurturing their gifts. Our Heavenly Father has embedded something unique inside all of us so all we need to do is nurture it. So, tell me, do you think you're up for the task? I think you are. No, I know you are. You are brilliant!

Approaching Competition

There are various ways to approach competition. As I stated before, you can either run with it, run past it, or run away from it. Your field will determine which one of these approaches works best for you. The "running-with-it approach" means co-existing, just working side by side. An example of this would be a teacher or a pastor. There's no competition in these fields (well, I don't think there is). Teachers teach in their respective fields, and pastors are responsible for shepherding their own churches. I think that this approach can be attributed to most industries, respectfully. I follow a lot of inspirational brands on social media, and they all seem to do fine just working alongside each other. I don't think they're too concerned about competition, and that's a beautiful thing.

If you're going to run past your competition, then, you better be the best. There are certain industries where to thrive, you have to be exceptional at what you do. A great example would be if you own a restaurant. Not only does your food need to be on point, but you need to have excellent customer service, a spotless facility—especially now. Your place also needs to be Instagram-ready, because you never know whose Instagram page it could end up on.

Lastly, running away from the competition means simply creating your own lane. You're not really running away from the competition, just creating your own lane beside it. This is the best approach for you if you're a creative. Creating your own lane is where the real gold is. Even if an industry is saturated, there is still room to create your own niche within it.

Where Competition Should End

There are some places where competition is not welcomed, and that is the church. There are no niches in the church and only one approach—to work *with* each other collectively as one body. This is a topic that needs its own book, but I cannot end this chapter without addressing the church. We should not be competing with each other as believers. Whether we are a business owner, a public figure, or whoever we are, we all play an important role in God's Kingdom. There is no room for arrogance here, and certainly no room for competition. If God needs to be in the details of every other aspect of life, then the same applies to the body of Christ.

The members of the church are the body of Christ, while the head of the Church is Christ. Just like your limbs and the bones in your body all work together, so does the church. With that said, the body of Christ does not compete with each other; we ought to work collaboratively. We have to learn to work together in the Church so that we can make real changes in the world. Imagine what we could do as the body if we all dropped our egos? If we were to use our brilliance along with the teachings of Christ, we would be unstoppable. Are you willing to drop your ego? There is no competition when it comes to doing God's work.

If we are going to approach competition like good stewards, we need to change our attitudes about competition. We all have a race to run but we must wear the shoes that fit us. We must be creative and strategic without letting our strategy become more important than our identity. As good stewards and God-fearing women, we all have one common goal—fulfilling our God-given purpose. Even more specifically, to push toward the upward call of Christ. Yes, we all have our own personal goals, but regardless, the most important goal we all share as believers is fulfilling God's purpose for our lives. We are brilliant people capable of creating our own lanes while working together at the same time. We don't compare ourselves to each other or to the world's standards. God has already set the standard so no need to waste time and energy trying to fit into anyone else's. We all have this desire to want to be better than the rest, the desire to fit in and win, but know this—you have already won the race. You just have to start running.

7

Clarifying Your Mission

I was listening to a podcast from a well-known and respected business coach with over 50k followers who decided to delete all of her products and start from scratch. She talked about how she was just fed up with the self-help industry and how oversaturated and tainted it has become. She's right! The industry has pretty much taken on a life of its own. She knew where she was, but most importantly, she knew where she wanted to go. She went on to say how she wanted to focus solely on giving people the proper value in whatever form that takes, even if it means starting over. She did it—she got clear about her mission. In order to show people what starting over looks like, she was humble enough to start over herself. Yes, she had over 50k followers, but even so, she took a risk by starting over and challenging the self-help industry, in general.

Would you be willing to start over no matter what stage you're in? Starting over is not easy. I started over myself in my thirties, leaving my cushy nine-to-five job and moving to another country, nothing easy about that!

We need to be clear about our mission, and the only way we're going to get clear is by being obedient to God's calling for our life. This is a hard one to follow, especially when you have to start over or when you see people who have built successful businesses without following God's plan. You see, there is this thing called free will that God gives us. It allows us to do what we want, but what are we doing with all this free will? We have to be mindful that there will come a day when we will have to answer for how we use it. In order to focus on where God is taking you, you'll need to learn to identify the cracks that are keeping you from gaining clarity. Cracks are anything that disrupts your path, like anxiety or misusing your free will. Even your own ego can get in the way. Anything that distracts you is a crack.

CRACKS IN OUR MISSION

I wrote a lot about that burning desire to be free in chapter 2, The Freedom Trap. Whether it's financial freedom, freedom to move here and there, or any other kind of freedom, it's a big part of why we start our own thing. Many of us want to run our own show, and that's understandable. However, if you'll remember, it's not just our show we're running. We are stewards, here to manage what God has given us. Whether it be in our careers, our businesses, and our lives, we all have a role to play in expanding the Kingdom agenda. Not accepting the real role we play as stewards is one of the biggest cracks in our mission. I'm not exempt from this either. I was always clear on my calling as a writer, however, my mission didn't always match my calling. The things I wanted to write didn't quite align with what God wanted me to write. My vision of what kind of writer I wanted to be was different from His vision. I had songs I had written that most certainly would not have been appropriate, screenplays I had to trash, and a whole book I was writing that I'm 100% sure would have been turned into a Netflix series.

But the more I drew closer to God, the more I knew I couldn't continue with these kinds of projects. The type of content I was writing was far from espousing godly principles, even if it was fiction. Here comes that voice of justification, *"I mean, it's fiction, they're just stories; it's not real."* I did the hardest thing ever—I scrapped everything. My screenplays and my book, all gone *(so sad!)*, and those spicy songs I wrote will never be produced. I'll tell you, that was not easy to do!

I know I'm not the only one who does this, trying to find ways to make disobedience work. I want to encourage you to stop trying to justify your actions. Justification fractures your mission.

You don't have to delete all your work like I did, but take the time to revise it if possible to be as God-honoring as it can be. As for me, the work I did was not salvageable, but I know I'm capable of producing these again but in the way God wants me to.

CRACKS IN OUR CHARACTER

Sometimes, we get in our own way. We have our own personality glitches that distort our mission. For me, it's anxiety. I have always struggled with social anxiety. Although I can't pinpoint exactly where it came from, if I had to guess, I would say it came from being badly bullied in my childhood. I stood up for myself by fighting— physically fighting, like boxing in-the-middle-of-the-street type of fighting. It wasn't until I became an adult that I realized I couldn't solve my problems by fighting anymore. That's when it happened. I believe it was that transition into adulthood of not knowing how to resolve things without it getting physical that led to my anxiety. I didn't know how to properly express myself and had no balance; I was either hot or cold.

When I got to college, it was all she wrote. I got a crash course on how things are to be handled, and I was not mentally prepared for this abrupt change. I became very shy and didn't know how to be assertive. My anxiety got the best of me. I had friends I would lose as soon as I befriended them. I didn't know how to interact with people, and, quite frankly, I had gotten to the point where I didn't want to. Nevertheless, I made myself look as normal as possible. Because of my anxiety, I went through a lot of unnecessary changes and was always searching to find comfort and inclusion as a way to remedy it. You might say that this was just normal college stuff, and, yes, it was a combination of both. But my anxiety was more troubling than the normal exploratory phases of being a college student.

My anxiety got so bad, it caused me to develop speech issues, then panic attacks and out-of-the-blue crying fits. I would be having a normal conversation with someone, then start tearing up. *Okay, maybe they won't notice. Just say it's your allergies.* I was not able to communicate effectively, causing me to suffer both personal and professional losses. I was in my own way. That job interview? Bombed it. Not speaking up for myself cost me relationships and self-respect, and being too shy and unassertive cost me connections that could have helped enhance my calling. Had I gotten a handle on all this early on, or at least talked to someone about it, I probably would have gotten to my calling a lot quicker.

Arrogance and Pride

Character glitches can cause fractures that play a big part in preventing you from seeing the bigger picture. We all have them. Arrogance is a major glitch, which is defined as "an exaggerated sense of one's own importance."[21] Arrogant people are cocky and unpleasantly proud of their accomplishments as if they achieved them on their own. Arrogance prevents people from getting the most out of their calling because they feel they've already arrived. Being arrogant is how you get stuck. If you are arrogant, your mission will never truly be complete if you are too proud of what you've already accomplished. Pride prevents you from getting the help you never thought you needed. You could be talking to someone who holds your next opportunity, but you're too proud to see how valuable they could be. You have not arrived; you still have a ways to go.

The problem with arrogance is that it clouds your judgment and makes you believe the world's perception of what is valuable, like status, money, and beauty. If a person you meet falls short of these things, your arrogance will keep you from giving them a chance. I could offer you a million dollars but if I don't meet your criteria, you might just tune me out. How can someone pour into a bowl that is already full? This is where the term "you're full of yourself" truly comes into play. You can't pour into an arrogant person, and most people wouldn't want to. It is a sort of passive self-sabotage that keeps you from building connections with genuine people who can really add value to your life. Romans 12:3 (NIV) tells us, "Do not think of yourself more highly than you ought, but rather think of yourself with sober judgment, in accordance with the faith God has distributed to each of you."

No one should think of themselves higher than they ought to because nothing we have belongs to us anyway. Every skill, talent, or resource we are using to build the life we want comes from God. But we are just renting space on Earth for a short period of time so we have to be careful how we are using our gifts. Most importantly, we have to consider how we treat people. Use your time here wisely and don't let your ego prevent you from seizing opportunities that may not be packaged the way you want it. I'm happy to say that I've never been an arrogant person and I've maintained a lot of valuable relationships because of it. I've been to networking events both in the US and abroad and met people from all walks of life. There were millionaires, models, and CEO's, and you wouldn't have known it unless they told you. They dressed plainly, spoke quietly, and made you feel like you were the most important person in the room. After talking to them, they all had this in common: they were the complete opposite of who you thought they would be.

'Your mission will never truly be complete if you are too proud of what you've already accomplished.

One thing was for sure, I could tell these people were clear on who they were and where they were going. The thing that was most striking about them was their willingness to learn from others. They were able to be poured into and wanted to hear what I had to say. It's funny because they didn't have to give me the time or day, and they gave me more of their time than anybody else. We can all use some help. Even the richest people in the world all had some form of help. The problem with arrogant people is they think they already got it in the bag. It's sad they don't even realize they are giving up so much because they can't see past their little bag. You might say it's just confidence, but no. Confident people are still willing to listen and are happy to learn from others no matter who they are. Most arrogant people don't even know they're arrogant; it's like a preexisting condition they don't know they have. Want to know if you are cocky or confident? This is how you can tell:

- You want to be liked by people. People who are arrogant need validation from people, specifically people who they feel are of high status.

- You prefer the company of the rich and well-to-do and take pride in being popular. I can understand wanting to be around people who are doing well but don't look to them for validation. When you do this, you set their validation above God's validation, making them your idol in the end.

- You're bossy and prefer to be seen as the leader. You like being the boss and being acknowledged as such.

- You're judgmental. You're always rolling your eyes and smirking. Your nonverbal game speaks for itself.

- You don't know how to fall back and follow. You do the most and like the attention.

- You're prideful. You take pride in your possessions, popularity, and worldly connections.

- Lastly, the biggest red flag of all is that it's almost impossible for you to take direction! Especially from people who you think are not on your level.

God may test your humility by making you take direction from others and sitting at tables with people you're not comfortable with.

When you are arrogant, you think you are untouchable, and that is very dangerous. Perhaps one of the clearest examples of how arrogance can be dangerous is how America was being managed during the 2020 Coronavirus pandemic. As this book was being written, *we were, and still are,* in a pandemic. There was also a racial uprising at the same time that you could call a revolution, caused by the brutal killing of yet another unarmed black man at the hands of a police officer. This caused national outrage and sparked protests around the world, spreading as far as Europe and Asia, starting a revolution in the midst of a world health crisis! It was a worldwide phenomenon; you couldn't look away. Protests, riots, and businesses burned to the ground, all while protestors walked around with masks on to protect themselves from a virus. It was really something for the history books. Perhaps the scariest part of all was having a president who didn't take any of it seriously. Arrogance and ego are big reasons why we were (and still are) in a state of emergency.

National and civil unrest are extreme examples of how serious things can get when arrogance takes over; it can get to be very dangerous. Arrogance can prevent you from seeing clearly, period, no matter who you are. When you can't see clearly, then you won't be able to make sound judgments, and you sure as heck won't be able to take direction. You just might find yourself in a mess that may take years to clean up. All people, leaders, everybody, no matter who you are, are not exempt from taking direction. *Even Jesus took direction.*

So please, take a step back and get over yourself. You cannot walk in your calling if you're arrogant. How can you listen to God if you can't listen to anyone else? You wouldn't even be able to hear Him. God is going to require you to come out of your comfort zone and do things that will test your humility. This sometimes involves taking direction from others and sitting at tables with people you're not comfortable with. This is how you build relationships with the right people. The people you're uncomfortable around might be the people you need to be around – it's all about being humble and having the right kind of energy around you. Meanwhile, arrogance attracts the wrong type of energy and will keep you in a cycle of building relationships with people who don't add to your life. If you are serious about your calling, then you're going to have to be comfortable being uncomfortable, period. Arrogance can kill dreams. It can hurt them before they even have a chance to form.

Managing Your Ego

Another character glitch is ego. Ego and arrogance are very similar, but there is a difference. While arrogance is defined as having or revealing an exaggerated sense of one's own importance or abilities, ego is a person's sense of self-esteem or self-importance. An example would be watching the behavior on busy city streets. Are you the person who moves out of the biker's way so you won't get hit? Or are you the one who gets offended when they signal you to move? They are trying not to hit you, that's why they are signaling you to move. There's nothing to prove here, but your ego will turn that experience into something more than it needs to be if you let it. I've seen people purposely not move out of someone's way just to see if they will bump them, saying things like, "I wish they would" or " I liked to see them try!" It really isn't that serious. Your ego is basically a collection of self-interest impulses and how you protect those interests.

Have you ever gotten offended when you gave someone a compliment and they didn't compliment you back? That is your ego talking as well as the spirit of offense rearing its ugly head. Maybe you are one of those who don't adapt well to change. These days, I think wearing a mask might be one of the biggest changes we've had to adapt to. People with sensitive egos view change as a challenge even if it is meant to protect them.

Handling Rejection

To build your mission, you have to learn how to deal with the word "no." I don't look at "no" as *never*; I just look at it as *next time*. Being told no is a part of the process of building your brand and is sometimes necessary to make room for the right opportunities. I happen to have grown fond of the word no, as it has saved me from getting locked into things that didn't serve me well. Imagine if you got a yes every time you wanted something? Would that really be a good thing? A combination of no's and yes's provides a necessary balance in your mission. I'll even use a harsher word, *rejection*. Rejection is just the harsh reality of being told no. Maybe you didn't get that part, or that job, or maybe a potential client decided to go with someone else. Whatever it is, rejection is a part of the process. One way that has helped my own ego is looking at the person who rejected me as another human who has probably been rejected themselves, because, well, they have. We all have been rejected at some point. If you can get over rejection, then you are already halfway there. We all have glitches or little nuances in our personality, but don't let it keep you from seeing the bigger picture. You don't have time to allow anything else to compromise your mission. Life is hard enough already.

'Your mission statement is your foundation, so
'whatever it is it should line up with godly 'principles.

Getting Clear on Your Mission

Have you ever been audited before? It's like the most nerve-wracking thing ever! Yes, Uncle Sam came for me, and I quickly learned not to take my affairs with the government lightly. One thing is for sure: don't take the details of your mission lightly either. To get clear on what the details should be, let's start with your mission statement. Take Chick-fil-A, for example. Their mission statement states, "To glorify God by being a faithful steward of all that is entrusted to us. To have a positive influence on all who come in contact with Chick-fil-A."

Your mission statement is your foundation, so whatever it is it should line up with godly principles. My mission statement says something like, "To use my God-given gifts of writing and content creation to inspire others, positively impact my audience, and add to the Kingdom."

Needs a little work but that about sums it up.

It's important to have a strong foundation to work from because we are being audited by the Most High. You have to ask yourself, "Is all that I am doing bringing glory to God?" He is auditing to see if you really are ready for what He has for you, or if He should pass it to someone else? Do you really want someone else to walk through the door meant for you? When God first revealed my identity as a writer, He revealed it through someone else He used as a vessel. Now that method of delivery couldn't have made it more clear.

The man didn't even say much. He just said, "Are you a writer? Are you writing something?" A very specific thing to ask someone, if you ask me. Mind you, this man didn't know a thing about me. After that experience, I went on to work on my own mission statement and have been holding myself to it ever since. I'm learning that God doesn't tell us things for no reason. No, He tells us these things in form of a revelation.

Writing was something I knew I needed to keep pursuing. Had I taken those revelations more seriously in the beginning, I'm sure I would have been successful a long time ago. I encourage you to ask God to show you where you've dropped the ball in your mission. It's through conviction that you will clearly see where you need improvement. When God revealed to that man that I was a writer, that's all I needed to feel convicted. From this place of conviction, you can work on crafting a mission statement that you can build from and things will become more clear. He will give you everything you need to move forward because, at the end of the day, your mission isn't just about you. It's much bigger than that. What will your mission statement say?

PART THREE

Executing

"AND HE SAID TO THEM ALL, IF ANY MAN WILL COME AFTER ME, LET HIM DENY HIMSELF, AND TAKE UP HIS CROSS DAILY, AND FOLLOW ME."

LUKE 9:23 KJV

8

Obedience.

I've had to give up a lot of things to pursue my calling. Has it been easy? Of course not. Being obedient is no walk in the park. However, I would have gone in a completely different direction as a writer if I hadn't been obedient. First off, this book would have never happened. Before this book, I was actually in the middle of writing a completely different one. It was a fiction book that had everything under the sun—sex, drugs, violence, profanity, all of the normal things you see. But as my relationship with the Lord strengthened, I knew I couldn't pursue it. That made me sad because I knew that book would have been so good, like movie-potential good. Even so, my conscience would have eaten me up putting that book out. Secondly, I still have dreams of being a songwriter, screenwriter, and possibly a filmmaker, but if I had remained on the world's side of things, I would have been a very different kind of writer. My songs would have most likely been sexualized R&B songs, and my screenplays would have fit right in with the New Age agenda.

I have so many things I've written that will never leave my computer now because they wouldn't have been acceptable or pleasing to the Lord. I swear I almost cried having to give up these projects. I felt like I missed an opportunity, but it had to be done. Luke 9:23, says, "And he said to them all, 'If any man will come after me, let him deny himself, and take up his cross daily, and follow me.'" We say we take God seriously, but it's all about action. What are you willing to give up to follow Him? Even though we have free will, we can't have one foot in the world and the other in God's Kingdom. Unfortunately, in today's culture, we've prioritized our free will over His will.

When you hear the word "obedience," how does it make you feel? Does it make you feel powerless? As women, we tend to associate this word with being submissive, another word that doesn't sit well, especially with women in today's world. Submission doesn't always sit too well with my rebel-like spirit either. Well, I've got news for you: obedience is a form of submission but not like the world may have you might think. Let me break it down for you.

Being obedient doesn't mean you're a puppet who has no free will. "Obedience" is defined as "Compliance with an order, request, or law, or submission to another's authority."[22] Let's unpack the word "submissive," which means "ready to conform to the authority or will of others; meekly obedient or passive."[23] You humbly conform to God's will but you still have your free will. Godly obedience is not about removing your free will; it is conforming (shaping) to *God's* will, utilizing your own free will while operating in His will. Got it? This is a word that will never get old no matter how much we think we've outgrown it, so we ought to get used to it. We'll never be too smart, too empowered, or too grown to be obedient.

'We'll never be too smart, too empowered,
or too grown to be obedient.

All that said, this chapter is going to be deep. We'll look at the issues we have around obedience as it relates to our calling. Obedience really is the key to achieving true success. When you are obedient to God's calling, you unlock opportunities that are far more rewarding than if you just followed your own path. As much as I wish it were true, there are no cutting corners. I want to illustrate the main areas where I think we drop the ball. We are spiritual people but not religious. We are religious people but not spiritual. We are mothers, daughters, sisters, entrepreneurs, influencers—we are many things. We are all at least one of those things. We are very busy, aren't we? We are all trying to build something, and it's beautiful. We are many things, but one thing we are not is obedient.

CULTURE

The first issue of disobedience relates to culture. In today's culture, we are the most liberated and free-spirited people we have ever been, so it's no surprise that being obedient is not popular. We are obsessed with freedom of expression and independence. You cannot tell someone to do anything without them feeling like they're forced to do so, even if it's for their own good. I have to agree—independence and being able to freely express myself is a wonderful feeling, and I'm all for it. However, I feel that we have become *too* independent. We've become so empowered that we've empowered God right out of everything. God has virtually no part of many of these belief systems and empowerment movements. Today's culture has become the queen of inclusivity of everything *except* God —more specifically, Jesus. You can't even say His name without someone giving you the side-eye.

Since God is not impartial and does not stand for partiality, you shouldn't be partially devoted to your purpose or Him.

Most unfortunate is that churches have this issue too. It's very hard for people to understand that if you are truly saved, you cannot be both of the world and God's Kingdom (James 1:8–10). We have to remember that God is not impartial and does not stand for partiality. Just like you don't want to be partially devoted to your purpose, you shouldn't be partially devoted to Him. I had to come to terms with this myself. I used to be your typical worldly Christian—drinking, smoking, partying on Saturday, then worshiping on Sunday. Yes, I was baptized and saved, but my lifestyle did not match my saved status. Back in the day, I remember going out, and if I saw a stage or even a table, it was only a matter of time before I was up there dancing in stilettos.

Culture makes it perfectly okay for this kind of grey area to exist. Can you have grey areas in your business? Grey areas exist in businesses where the border between legal and illegal is fuzzy. You shouldn't operate in a grey area in business, and you certainly shouldn't operate in grey areas with God. We have made culture the truth and have put biblical principles in the "old, traditional" category, and what a mess this has made. The world wants to redefine everything, and even the slightest opposition to it will get you canceled. This is what disobedience looks like. I swear, I get anxious just thinking about all the things I cannot say.

TRADITION VS. TRUTH

The second issue with disobedience has to do with another issue in today's culture is following tradition versus the truth of God's Word. For black people, because of our harsh history of oppression, it's no surprise we have a strong desire to want to know our truths and reclaim our past traditions. Respectfully, we should. We have a right to know, so much has been kept from us. However, I am noticing now more than ever that we have put the desire to know our own truth over the desire to know God's truth. Proverbs 3:5–6 (KJV) says, "Trust in the Lord with all thine heart; and lean not unto thine own understanding. In all thy ways acknowledge him, and he shall direct thy paths."

A great majority of our history has been suppressed, and now that we are learning more about it, it's causing us to question everything—even God. This is to be expected from a people who have been scarred as much as we have but make no mistake, God is not to blame for this confusion. If anything, if we have questions about His creation, then we need to lean toward the Creator for the answers, "Turn to God and he will reveal the truth to you."

The other issue with tradition vs. truth is it has become trendy to embrace our newfound cultural traditions and do away with traditions we feel are outdated as we learn more about our own history. One of the best examples of tradition vs. truth is how we view the Bible. We've put the Bible in the "outdated, traditional" box instead of the "truth" box. One of the most controversial conversations around this topic is the act of slaveowners cherry-picking the Bible to justify their treatment of slaves and slavery, in general.

Millennials, especially, have adopted this view the most. According to an article from Christianity Today, the urban culture sees Christianity as an

If we have questions about His creation, then we need to lean toward the Creator for the answers,

Anglo-dominated religion that isn't sensitive to the issues of black and brown people, and, therefore, finds African traditional religions more alluring. However, they often fail to realize that Christianity has existed in Africa so long that it can be considered an indigenous religion, especially in Northern Africa. "The similarities to the Christian faith are so strong that theologian John Mbiti describes the God of the Bible as 'none other than the God who is already known in the framework of traditional African religiosity.' Consequently, it wasn't a quantum leap for our enslaved ancestors to transition to Christianity; rather, it was a logical step forward because they were prepared by their existing theological system."[24]   The truth is, Christianity has been a part of African culture long before the European slave trade took place. We have the apostles Mark and Paul to thank for the spreading of Jesus's ministry in Northern Africa.

It's a shame that parts of the Bible were used incorrectly to justify such horrible acts, however, I don't want this to be your focus. Instead of discounting the Bible altogether, ask God to help you make sense of it. I would encourage you to lean toward God to direct your path instead of leaning toward your emotions.

A good example of what leaning toward your emotions looks like is something I saw while scrolling through Twitter one day that really disturbed my spirit. Social media tends to have that effect sometimes. The post stated, "Who did we pray to before slavery?" What made it so bad was that it was printed on a shirt in bold letters. We are hurt and have a lot of trust issues, and quite frankly, who could blame us? Our ancestry has been hidden from us for many years, not taught in schools, and not included in mainstream curriculums, so we tend to attack anything that interferes with us learning about our history, including Christianity.

The same God we serve today has always been a part of our culture. He has not changed, but because we are so hungry to embrace our heritage, how we relate to Him has. We are leaning more toward our cultural findings and using them to help form our own truth. I get it, we want to reclaim our traditions; however, while learning about our heritage, we should include learning the Gospel as well. You would be surprised at the connection you'll find. It's not the theology I want you to focus on. What I really want you to understand is that God deserves the credit and attention more than our traditions, culture, and so forth. Don't make culture an obsession, even if it is a part of your heritage. We have to watch this. When we obsess over our culture, we make it our idol.

So, if you are asking, how did culture become a form of disobedience? It's because we value it over the truth. We value it over the Gospel, and, ultimately, over our relationship with God. There's a reason why the belt of truth is the first piece of the Armor of God that Paul mentions in Ephesians 6:10–18. The truth holds everything together. Without it, all things fall apart.

Setting an Example of Obedience

As Christians and people of God, we are not setting good examples of what obedience looks like. Last summer, I went to a very uplifting networking event. Everything went so right with the event except one part that made me uncomfortable, the prayer. Yes, out of everything that went right, the prayer made me uncomfortable. Why? I could tell that this woman, as beautiful as the prayer was, did not want to offend anyone, so she prayed a *safe* prayer. We were at the kind of event where saying the name *Jesus* was most likely taboo, so she concluded the prayer without saying it. Like I said before, people will give you the side-eye in a minute if you say the name, Jesus. Now I can't confirm the real reason why she omitted Jesus's name, but I do see a lot of Christians doing this. I figured she omitted it because she did not want to offend anyone. For Christians, this is how we seal our prayers, and it's not up for discussion.

What I can confirm is that we live in a culture where we are so afraid of offending people that we are willing to deny ourselves to make other people feel comfortable as if our own peace of mind doesn't matter too. We can't keep acting like this kind of thing isn't a problem. You might say, "Well, what's the big deal? It's just a minor detail." Matthew 10:33 makes it a big deal. Jesus says, "But whoever denies me before men, I also will deny before my Father who is in heaven." Not only is leaving Him out a form of denial, but Jesus warns us that nobody can get to the Father but by Him (John 14:6). Not sealing a prayer in Jesus's name might seem like you are omitting a small detail, but I'm here to

*Learn to be led by the Spirit instead
of other people's opinions.*

tell you the details matter, and Jesus is a detail you do not want to leave out. It's funny how we are so resistant to Christ but willing to take risks with everything else in the world. Friends, we have to learn to be more unapologetic about uplifting Christ. Making other people comfortable has become the priority, so we need to learn to be led by the Spirit instead of other people's opinions. Jesus is essential. Obedience requires you to acknowledge that.

DISOBEDIENCE IN THE CHURCH

This is a big one. The current culture of the Church has become too relaxed and has made it okay to have a grey area. I've been to churches feeling like I just left a concert. This is one of the reasons many millennials lack interest in the church; they don't know what obedience looks like because we look like the world. Churches these days are more centered on using their own methods to attract members instead of letting God use them to win souls. They see us say one thing and do another. The lack of cultural representation in churches does not help either. It adds to their distaste for the church. These are reasons why if they do go to church, they are most likely to leave the way they came, and well, could you blame them? They end up firmly placing the church in that "old, traditional" box instead of the "truth" box.

If we are not obedient ourselves, then what message is that sending to this generation? They will end up redefining it for themselves, and they have. They've started movements, brands, trends that don't include God. Hypocrisy has pushed them away, which is a big problem. Building a brand without the guidance of the church is possible, and a lot of women are, unfortunately, encouraging others to embrace this idea.

I can go on and on about this, but that is for another book. The point is, God's agenda for the Church is clear. We just have to figure out how to work together to execute it so that people will take us seriously and won't leave the same way they came.

Once the Church gets rid of the grey areas, then it could be an even more powerful resource for ministry on all levels of personal, spiritual, and professional development.

Operating Outside the Will of God

The lines are very blurred these days, and this is the reason why Christians are not taken seriously. When we operate in grey areas, we operate outside the will of God. As hard as this may be to believe, God's principles are simply black and white, not grey. You can blur them if you want if that makes you feel more comfortable, but it's still going to be what it is. It's confusing when right and wrong become the same thing. It's confusing when the "Universe" and "God" mean the same thing. *Yes, that's a thing now.* We are so confused, so why does it surprise us that the next generation after us is also confused?

This liberating "do-whatever-I want" thing feels too good to let go of because we have no idea what it means to be a good steward. A lot of us have never even heard of the term. I get it; it's a new age, and we have to get with the times. But all of this (everything) still belongs to God no matter what we change. Cultural norms, family structure, even government...guess what? God created all of it. When you make it about you, when you make it about culture, that's when things start to fall into the enemy's hands. On an episode of Dr. Tony Evans's Urban Alternative podcast, Dr. Evans gave a brilliant explanation where if you rent a house and paint it, that still won't make it your house no matter what coat of paint you put on it. God started it and He will be the one to finish it. Therefore, He should always be the one you seek first before making decisions.[25]

So, how do you know if you are operating in grey areas? Time for another audit, let's go!

1. *Audit God.* Ask yourself, what kind of God is He? Scripture will provide more than enough responses to that question. Write down what you think His characteristics are and allow

Him to reveal Himself to you. Doing this will make you more aware of His character, thus making you more aware of His expectations.

2. *Audit your audience.* What do people say about you? What do your customers say about you? Are you changing lives by making people feel better? Who are the people you see gravitating to you the most? It's true what they say—you can tell a lot about a person by the company they keep, and you can tell a lot about your business by the kind of customers you have.

3. *Audit yourself.* Here is where you can carefully take account of your thoughts, words, and actions. Is the word of God included in your daily routine? How often do you pray and meditate on His Word?

Rules

Why are we not comfortable following rules? Rules are not made to make you submissive; they are created to make society more ordered. I know this is hard. Even a free-spirited person, like myself, has trouble accepting this, because we don't like being told what to do. However, we need rules and regulations in every aspect of our lives. Just think how chaotic things would be if we all did whatever we wanted. With the COVD-19 pandemic combined with the 2020 protests, we got to see chaos in real-time, giving a front-row seat of what disobedience causes on a larger scale. Sadly during this time, a lot of businesses closed their doors for good—no one saw any of this coming. One could only imagine how things would be now if people really did let go and let God.

> *"The closer God is to a government and its citizens, the more ordered the society will be; the further God is from a government, the more chaotic the society will become."*[26]

> – Dr. Tony Evans

The same goes for your career path, your brand, or your business. The more God is woven into the foundation, the better off it will be.

Allowing Perfection to Stall Us

You will never be perfect, so just begin, sis, let's go! I have always been an overachiever, but I'm starting to realize that God doesn't want perfection; He just wants us to be obedient. He wants us to get out of our comfort zone and walk in faith. In business, there is always a process, a way we are used to doing things to get results. We must have pretty pictures, that pretty logo, trendy business cards, all of that before we proceed, but God is saying, "JUST DO IT!" Stop trying to be perfect. If you are waiting until you are 100% sure, then you will never get there.

Walking by faith requires you to begin even when you're only 50% sure. Go to that convention, snag that speaking engagement, and just do it! I'm not saying be unprepared, but you don't need everything to be pretty and perfect before starting. Perfection is the enemy's way of keeping you from moving forward. If you think about it, God's way is much easier than our way anyway. With our way, we spend too much time and money trying to be perfect, while God's way is just as simple as trusting Him. Exodus 4:12 (KJV) says, "Now therefore go, and I will be with thy mouth, and teach thee what thou shalt say." Go and speak, that's it! Having faith doesn't always come easy, I know, but work on it a little each day and you'll see the difference.

Make Time for God

Just like we make time for everything else, we can make time for Him. I get it, life is busy and distracting, but make time to read and pray so you can see clearly where He is leading you. No distractions, just you and Him. This way you can see what He wants you to do, not what you think He wants you to do. You must make sure you're not taking part of the plan and running with it when God has

God doesn't want ⸱perfection,
He ⸱just wants us to be obedient.

so much more to add to the plan. If God is not involved in your routine, then God is not involved in *your* plan. Your plan becomes just that, *your* plan.

Here are a few suggestions:

- Spend time with God in prayer, and He will lead you to the resources that are more suited for you. These resources may be in the form of books, a coach, a connection on social media, a therapist—resources can come in many forms.

- Read God's Word daily. One of my favorite books in the Bible is the book of Proverbs. This book, derived from the wise sayings of King Solomon, is an outstanding book about wisdom. It speaks on a multitude of subjects from money to parenting to friendship and is one of the best books on obedience. I hear people talk about Scripture being outdated, but a lot of the teachings are common knowledge and common sense. It shouldn't matter how old it is. I encourage you to get familiar with Proverbs.

- Last, but not least, go on a fast. All business owners and entrepreneurs alike should fast! Listen, fasting is a powerful tool and an even more powerful weapon against the enemy. It can be tough, but this is how you can really get God to move on your behalf. When God sees you sacrificing something you're attached to for Him, He will make a way for you, and I promise you, it will blow you away! Out of all the things you can do for your business and for yourself, fasting should be at the top of your list.

A Challenge for You

I challenge you to keep God in the details by getting out of your comfort zone. Do things you normally wouldn't do and go to places you normally wouldn't go. We challenge ourselves by putting ourselves out there when we build our brands and businesses, so now it's time to execute God's plan for our brands and businesses the same way. It's time to be good stewards. Hone your skills and be well-rounded, but don't lose sight of your foundation. Second Peter 1:10 (KJV) says, "Wherefore the rather, brethren, give diligence to make your calling and election sure: for if ye do these things, ye shall never fall."

We have no problem taking from God, but we don't allow Him to do the work in us that needs to be done. When you allow Him to work, you won't believe the things you would be able to do with your gifts. However, our automatic response is to lean into what makes us comfortable. It may make us uncomfortable to stand up for God in public or in environments where God is clearly not welcomed. It may make us uncomfortable to post a Bible verse on our page knowing the possibility of losing followers, but you can't let that stop you. We are so concerned about not offending people that we either recognize part of God or we omit Him altogether.

We are to be ambassadors for Christ, and that requires us to be all in. One of the most common phrases I hear people say is, "Go and get what God has for you." This phrase is used so loosely. It's a blanketed message used by almost every coach, entrepreneur, and influencer. There is more to God than getting what He has for you. God is not a gift dispensary. Stop reducing Him to a vending machine of gifts and favors. No, ma'am, He is not that. As Tony Evans would say, "He is not your spiritual Santa Claus." You can reference and quote God all day but that's not enough.

Using God to complement your brand, but rejecting everything else about Him, is something that has never sat well with me.

'We are to be ambassadors for Christ,
and that requires us to be all in.

I hope you see now why being obedient is so important. When you decide to go after the plans God has for your life, you are in new territory. When you are in new territory, you cannot operate the way you used to. You cannot operate the way the world does, either.

There will be challenges, but you cannot let what other people think to keep you from conquering those challenges the right way. As hard as it may be, you must surrender. I did just that and haven't looked back since. I dropped to my knees and said "Lord, I'm done. You can have me, all of me. I want what you have for me so I promise I will serve you for the rest of my life." I prayed about it, and I even wrote my official surrender date in my journal "10/04/2020."

I've come to terms with the fact that I needed to completely let go of my own plans years ago but wasn't at the point of completely surrendering. I just wasn't ready, because you never make a promise to God unless you plan on following through with it, and that has always scared me (Ecclesiastes 5:5). It took some personal trials and tribulations and a mental breakdown that came out of nowhere in the middle of a pandemic to get me to the point of making such a promise. Now, my plans and God's plans are the same plans, and it's a beautiful thing. We are on the same page now. I've found that the more time you spend with God, the more you want to do right by Him. I don't even have the taste for a lot of things I used to do in the past.

I know this is heavy stuff, but know this: Your obedience does not go unnoticed, and God rewards those who are. If you stick to His plans for you, you will be rewarded so much so that you won't even be able to handle all the blessings He has for you. Imagine that! You've got the skills and talents—just imagine how powerful you could be if you are obedient.

9

Marketing

You are a gem, and I know you can't wait to show the world. I would say that the world can't wait for you. Remember when I spoke about brilliance? We've all got something that's going to wow people. No matter how small we think it is, somebody's going to love it, and someone is going love you. You just need to make sure that what you put out is God-approved. If you've read this far, by now you should know why that's so important. Being about one thing and doing another won't fly anymore. Be careful of the image you portray. Everything I've discussed in the previous chapters comes down to this—it's time to wrap your gift and present it to the world and make sure you're successful while you're at it.

BRANDING

It should be easy for someone to tell that God is woven into the foundation of your business. Whether it be your logo, your mission statement, the way your facility is decorated, and down to the way you look, your branding should reflect that you are a woman of God. With that, your customers should already know what to expect.

What's even more important is how you conduct yourself. There was a popular quote circulating on social media that sums this up beautifully, "Your smile is your logo, your personality is your business card, how you leave others feeling after an experience becomes your trademark." This couldn't be more accurate. The way you conduct yourself should clearly show that God is in you. The goal should be that when someone spends time with you, they should leave feeling better than they did when they arrived. Now let's get to the specifics of branding.

Colors

One of my favorite parts of marketing is branding, what should your brand look like? Formally trained in this area with a post-grad degree in Interactive Media Management, where content strategy and design was the main focus, I've gained an immense amount of knowledge in the area of design and content creation. I've also worked in the digital marketing industry for about six years and understand that branding is everything. Even with all the formal training and experience, combined with the fact the industry changes frequently, I learn something new every day.

The first thing is colors. There should be at least three colors in your brand, no more than four. For example, black, white, and blue, so two primary and one accent color to start. It is industry standard to have two primary colors and one or two accent colors. It also looks cleaner and more sophisticated. I would also recommend using light colors and preferably not shooting on a dark background. Of course, this depends on your brand. White looks good on black, for example, but a rule of thumb is not to make things too dark; lighter colors are more appealing to the eye.

It's also important to understand that certain colors provoke certain emotions. There is a reason financial and healthcare industries use blues and greens. Colors influence how people feel. According to an article on colors and branding, neuroscientist Antonio Damasio said, "Your brand colors have the ability to impact your sales or performance even more than the products you offer."[27]

Fonts

This is also the same idea for fonts. There is a psychology behind the type of font you use. You also don't want to use too many. I always recommend using no more than three. If you use too many different fonts, it looks messy and confusing. Dress up your website and social media just like you would if you had a store. Colors, fonts, placement of text all make an impression on people. If you don't know what fonts to use, no worries. Myfonts.com is a good resource for fonts, as well as Google fonts and Adobe fonts. These services have very large font catalogs, so it can be overwhelming. Some of these have price tags attached to them, which could be worth it, but if not, just simply use the free fonts you like that come with whatever design program you're using. My suggestion would be to stick with a Sans Serif font and one script font (cursive), which should only be used for accent purposes or a logo. Do not use script font as your main font for your copy.

Usability

Next is usability. This is one of the main focuses of my grad program—you can make it pretty, but does it work? You should be asking yourself the following questions:

Is it easy for someone to find the shopping cart on my website?

How long does it take for someone to find what they're looking for?

Is my site mobile-friendly? (Everybody uses their phone to shop these days.)

With usability, there needs to be a three-step process: click the product or service, add to cart, then checkout—that's it. There shouldn't be a bunch of steps in between. You have to remember, again, this isn't just about you; it's about your audience.

There's a saying that goes in marketing: make it easy for people to do business with you.

There's a saying that goes in marketing: make it easy for people to do business with you. You could be the nicest person in the world with the best products, but if it's difficult for your customers to do business with you, they will be turned off, and it will be harder for you to grow. You need to design things in a way that keeps the customer (the end-user) in mind.

A Clear Message

Last is clarity. Ask yourself, what problem am I solving? Is it clear to my customers what I do? Who are my customers anyway? What do they look like? The best way to determine this is to create avatars. Avatars are customer profiles that have the characteristics of your target market. It would include information like age, race, interests, and other demographic information. Here's how to create one.

Use a picture of someone who looks like your target market. Include their age, gender, marital status, and any other information you feel is important in determining your audience. For example, let's say you sell personalized planners that are on the pricier side. You would first ask yourself, *Who is willing to pay $60 for a planner?* When you do your research, your avatar might be a young woman between the ages of 28 to 36, who lives in cities where the income might be a bit higher, like New York, Atlanta, or Los Angeles. She might be single, have no kids, and be a college grad making at least $45k a year.

You may not be able to get these exact statistics, but the point is when you get the information in front of you, you'll have a much clearer view of who your customers are. Maybe you sell Christian planners or planners that have a theme. Then the data you collect would need to be specifically tailored toward that market.

So, who would be your ideal clients? Who would be the best candidates for your services? My target market has always been small businesses and personal brands, but I've learned over time to be even more specific than that. It didn't take long for me to figure out who my primary audience was. Most of us have a general idea of our customers, like gender and age, but you need to narrow it down even more. Depending on your business, you may even have to consider using more sensitive characteristics like political status and race.

Figuring out the problem you're solving should be done before you even start designing a logo. Let's say you live in a community that's predominately vegan and green living, and you see that the one thing this community doesn't have is natural hair care products. This may be a great time to start a small vegan hair care line specifically for this community. Eventually, you may want to expand but just focus on trying to fill a void.

Getting clear about what you do comes down to the connection between your solution and your target market. It needs to be clear that what you offer is the best solution for the problem for the market you are selling to. This is why you can't be all over the place with your messaging. For instance, a life coach and a business coach are two different professions, similar but different. Even though they are both coaches, the details in their messaging must be different.

One of the rules in marketing is that when you give people too many choices, they are less likely to buy.

A life coach's message may be more for personal development, giving examples of personal life experiences, like trauma or focusing on emotional health. A business coach may have some personal things in there, but the focus is more on professional development and business advice. Being clear means being specific about what you offer, ensuring that you will be able to give the best results.

This brings me to the related issue of offering multiple services. If you are someone who offers multiple services, I would say be careful with that. Offering too many products or services can confuse the buyer. I can attest to this myself, having fled from one place to another because of indecision. I was just too overwhelmed, so I ended up going somewhere else. A good example would be if you have a boutique, maybe offer a small number of products, say five products to start with. One of the rules in marketing is that when you give people too many choices, they are less likely to buy.

SOCIAL MEDIA

This is the fun but hardest part. If people want to check you out, you better believe they're going to social media first. Everything is front-facing here, meaning all of your content is visible to your audience, so all of your mistakes will be too. My grad teacher once told me this after making a small grammatical error on a blog I had written, "On the back end you are allowed to make some mistakes, while in front-facing roles, you cannot, period." I have always held myself to this principle. This feedback was harsh but necessary.

Throughout my time developing my career in marketing, l saw a harsh reality come to light. The harsh reality was that one hiccup could send me to the unemployment line or back to call center land. Your brand is always being audited by your audience. You never know who is watching you or the reason why they are watching you, so you need to be on point.

People may genuinely like your product or service or may refer you to someone else who's looking for your type of service. There may be opportunities where someone may be looking at you as a good fit for their brand and invite you for an interview. Remember, there is always someone with the power to bless you, so first impressions are very important. Look at social media as your first impression, and be careful about misspellings, grammatical errors, colors, and how you engage with your audience.

In the same respect, you need to have a plan and be careful what you post. Here is my rule of thumb when it comes to creating content:

Educate them, inspire them, and make them laugh.

You can post about current events too, but just use sound judgment when doing so. The point is to create content that will attract the right followers because, let's be honest—you want people who are going to eventually spend money with you not just find you intriguing. This works the same way in business. It's better to place more of your focus on nurturing the small number of quality customers you have than to focus on getting new ones who will likely try your product only once then flee. Don't get me wrong; you want your business to grow so you do want new customers, but just remember it's always quality over quantity. The small group of quality customers is more likely to recommend your product and tend to be more loyal over the larger group that just finds you interesting. This is how you grow organically, which would be a gamechanger for your business. Your loyal customers are who you want to nurture the most because they are the ones who transform businesses into household names.

Another thing to consider regarding social media is which platforms are the most valuable for your business. Let's break down each one.

Instagram

Instagram is a visual storytelling platform best used for posting images and videos. The primary age range is 18–29. If you are going to last here, then ensuring your content is high-quality and relevant is going to be very important to receive high engagement, which will help you have a longer life span on the platform. Consider investing some time into using Instagram reels as well.[28]

YouTube

With about two billion users, ages ranging from 18–34, there are a multitude of benefits from using this robust platform. You can easily reach an audience by creating your own videos and by advertising on other people's videos.[29] Another big benefit is that YouTube is very SEO friendly. SEO meaning "search engine optimized," which means if your videos are tagged correctly, you have the potential to rank higher in Google search results. Over 90% of all Google searchers click on the first ten organic results, and research has shown that for professional services and general companies, if you are driving traffic to a landing page—a page that captures a customer's information, with a video of yourself or company spokesperson speaking about your product or service, it can dramatically increase your list of leads and sales.[30] You can also make serious money by using Google AdWords and AdSense to make some money back from your video campaigns by allowing others to advertise on your videos.[31] I would suggest setting some time aside to learn more about how YouTube can help your business because it could be worthwhile.

Twitter

Twitter is a conversational platform wildly used by millennials and very much a world of its own. The best way to use this platform is to use real-time news or whatever is trending as a tool to advocate for your business. To get noticed here, discuss or comment on trending content but do so respectfully. Twitter has a way of reeling you into controversy if not used correctly. The primary age range is between 18–34 as of April 2021.[32]

Facebook

Despite all the controversy that surrounds Facebook, it can still be beneficial in building your business. It's a great space to build communities and private groups which helps your customers better interact with you once you've caught their attention. People value private groups because it gives them access to exclusive information and to have a more personalized experience with your brand.[33] I recommend running ads but not often as it can get expensive quick. Facebook is still valuable, but be mindful of what you post as Facebook has gotten stricter over the years and your account could get suspended at a moment's notice. I've had it happen to me several times, and it's a pain to resolve it. Internationally, 72.8% of users are between the 18–44 age range.

WhatsApp

WhatsApp is, in my opinion, one of the most underrated yet valuable messaging platforms. As in instant messenger, WhatsApp allows you to quickly respond and establish quicker communication, making it the perfect place to privately connect with your audience, and it's free! Research shows that SMS open rates are as high as 98% and 45%, compared to just 20% and 6% of all emails.[34] And, on average, it takes 90 seconds for someone to respond to a text and 90 minutes to respond to an email.[35] I know of a lot of real estate and financial literacy influencers that use this space very well. As of the third quarter of 2020, WhatsApp is used mostly by users between the ages of 26–35.[36]

Continuing with social media trends, some attention needs to be given to newer platforms, like TikTok, Clubhouse, Twitter Spaces, and Instagram Reels, just to name a few.

CONTENT

So what should you create? This is where it gets tricky for us Christians who try to be hip and godly at the same time. Ask yourself the following? Is what I'm doing glorifying God? Am I going to attract the right kind of attention? If you answered "yes" to both, then you're in the clear!

The number one type of content to create is videos. Videos are no doubt the fastest way to grow your following. You should be uploading at least one video a week. It can be a promo, a video introducing yourself, or a CTA, which is getting someone to do more than just like your post. The way our minds work, we are more likely to stop for a second longer when we see something moving— *it's a psychological thing.* People aren't interested in just looking at pictures anymore. They want something more engaging, more interactive. Look at what's happening with social media right now. You've got talk shows like Red Table Talk on Facebook, IG live shows, and one of the most innovative brands to date, Verzuz, a brand that was birthed on Instagram during the pandemic that features live collaborations between music artists. You don't have to do anything this big. I just want you to think big. This is what entertainment looks like these days. If the first couple of seconds is attractive enough to hold someone's attention, they may stick around longer.

What do I mean by attractive? Content that fits into the three categories I previously mentioned—inspiring, funny, and educational. Using eye-catching colors, like yellows and greens, and using a nice quality camera is also not a bad idea.

Quotes are always a nice touch too, but when you use them, make them bold and powerful. One of my favorite quotes I ever posted simply said this, "I lack nothing," in bold letters. I don't even think I wrote a caption, and it was very well received.

The next thing you need to do is get personal, so smile for the camera! Post pictures of yourself with a caption with a CTA. Calls to action are posts that get people to take action. They are essential in marketing because these are the types of posts that get comments and increase engagement. Don't be afraid to let your audience know what you need from them. An example of a CTA post would be, "What is the one area of your business you need the most help in? Drop in the comments below!"

Lastly, freebies. Plan to create an awesome freebie to give away, like a free eBook or e-Guide. These are very valuable and give your customers or clients a little preview of what's to come if they work with you. This is also the perfect way to build your email list.

What Shouldn't You Post?

As for what not to post, I am not a big fan of flyers, and Instagram isn't either unless you are running paid ads. Even though they are necessary sometimes, keep in mind that flyers don't get great engagement since the Instagram algorithm changed. And by the time this book comes out, it will have changed again. Instagram will only show your flyer to a small percentage of your followers because, guess what, they would rather you pay them to promote it instead. So, don't spend a ton of time creating pretty flyers unless you plan on spending money for a promoted post. Flyers only work well if you have a dedicated following or a private group on Facebook, for instance.

Tech

If you're like me, tech is my weak spot. I have to stop myself from spending money here. God is working on me! You only need a few tools to get started. Start with these: a graphic design tool, an email marketing tool, and a social media manager. Here are some tools that I've used over the years in my career and while building my own personal brand.

For graphic design, I use Photoshop and Canva. Canva is free and makes it super easy to create social media posts from scratch, no advanced graphic design skills are needed, just some patience and creativity. There is a paid version for Canva that gives you access to more cool design tools and templates. Photoshop is not free and not entirely necessary. I just use it because I've been using it for years. For social media management, I use a scheduling software called "Later." Later is a free social media manager that allows you to schedule and auto-publish your posts. This way you don't have to worry about posting manually. Perhaps one of the best social media management goodies I've ever come across is a platform called Iconosquare. It provides the most in-depth analytics out of any social media tool I've come across. For email marketing, I recommend Constant Contact. If you are just starting out and need something to help you get started, then Mail Chimp would be good for a beginner. They offer a free version of up to a certain number of contacts. If you are past the beginning stages and are ready to ramp up your business, I would suggest a new marketing tool that just came on the market called Groove Funnels. Groove Funnels is an all-in-one marketing platform that includes not only email marketing but creating ads, landing pages, and websites. This is what I am using for one of my businesses, and it works seamlessly. Another highly-rated email marketing tool is Klayvio. This tool is probably the best one to use if you sell a physical product, especially if you have a Shopify store. It syncs with Shopify beautifully and pulls in all your stats for you.

For your Instagram bio, I recommend using one of my favorites called lnk. bio. It allows you to use pictures, giving your links a more professional look. To keep yourself organized, I recommend using Trello, a fantastic task management system. For communication purposes, something like Slack is great for instant messaging and sharing files, or simply downloading WhatsApp is perfect for faster instant messaging purposes. All the tools I mentioned here have either free versions or a trial, so try them before emptying your pockets.

Maintenance

Now that you are up and running, you must maintain your business. This is where you hire that assistant or accountant. The tools I discussed above would also need to be in place to ensure everything is as seamless as possible, which will make it easier for your assistant to do their job if you hire one. Your social media posts should be scheduled, your email marketing should be turned on, everything you need to intake customers should be in automation mode. This way you can focus your attention on your product or services without having to do all the marketing legwork yourself. You need to have measures in place in case you're away so things are still able to run smoothly. Whether it's outsourcing or hiring a full-time assistant, do what's necessary to keep the engine running. At this stage, hiring a coach or a consultant could be helpful as well.

Another way you can maintain your business is by joining communities. There are plenty of Facebook groups and online communities that offer a great support system for other like-minded people who have similar goals and interests. I have joined a few of these groups on Facebook, and they can be very helpful. Joining these communities is how I also landed some of my first clients. If you have a problem in your business, trust and believe there is someone else that has experienced that same problem. Don't think you have to do it all on your own. No one, not a millionaire or even a billionaire, not even the Oprah's or the Jeff Bezos's of the world, has ever built anything alone. Are you building a business or are you building an empire? The level of maintenance depends on the size of your business and the size of your dream.

ADDING VALUE

Value is giving someone a reason to keep coming back to you or keep buying your products. Value also gives them a reason to tell somebody else about you. Adding value starts with putting yourself out there. First of all, you are already valuable, you just need to begin. Here's how you add value to potential and existing clients or customers.

Better buying options. If you have a product, offer free shipping or priority shipping, and accept a variety of payment options from PayPal, Gpay, and all major credit cards. Give customers the option to receive text confirmations as well. Also, if you have a Shopify store, there is an app called Shop that makes it incredibly easy to track packages, get updates, and more. Offer them discount codes and give them free access to your VIP program. If you don't have a VIP program, start one.

Start a podcast. Podcasts have proven to be very valuable outlets. I have made several connections and purchases from podcasts. A lot of podcasters, through their collaboration with other brands, offer discount codes to their listeners, which I've found to be incredibly valuable. But this isn't the only reason they are valuable. The information you can give your audience might compel them to purchase from you even more turning them into the organic customers I talked about. Podcasts usually have their own set of dedicated followers who are more than happy to spread the word about who they've been tuning in to.

Write a book. If you can't write, hire a ghostwriter if you can afford it. Or try writing it yourself with the help of a good editor. The book doesn't have to be 200 pages; it can be a small fifty-page book. I would say give the first few copies away for free with a purchase or maybe have a contest. If you are in the personal or professional development space, such as coaching or consulting, this could help your business tremendously. Plus, you can garner some residual income from your books because you only had to create them once and they will be up for sale for a long time. Books have a way of validating your expertise and can serve as a "business card," opening the door for more opportunities.

Surprise them. Offering surprise samples with a purchase can be the perfect touch to developing loyalty and goodwill among your customers. People appreciate value adds like freebies very much. Surprising them with a birthday gift would work too because, hey, who doesn't like these kinds of surprises?

Free events. I love when businesses do this. It's a fun way to promote themselves and build customer trust and loyalty. This may be further in the future, but you can do a free popup event with food trucks, free samples, and music. These days with the pandemic, virtual events may be more appropriate.

What bold and beautiful thing will you do for your business?

Creativity wins. Let me share something with you my church did that I thought was beautiful. They shot a video of the praise dancers dancing not in the church but outside in a public space. This is another form of marketing and dance ministry in its purest form. It was bold, they flowed freely, and piqued people's interest. There was no way they could be ignored. It was another form of street ministry. This way people would ask, "What are you doing?" "Who are you guys?" What a bold and beautiful way to attract members! What bold and beautiful thing will you do for your business?

If you take your calling seriously, the opportunities that will come your way will surely exceed your expectations. That's what God does—He exceeds expectations, so don't be afraid to put yourself out there. Easier said than done, I know, but just take it day by day, moment by moment. He will open doors for you that you never thought you were qualified to open. You don't have to spend a lot of money to market yourself either. There are so many free tools out there to use. You can just do an Instagram live to get started. You never know, that's all it might take to catch someone's attention.

Keep going, persevering in all you do. You never know—you might get the attention of some very important people and land some amazing opportunities! A book deal, a talk show, who knows the awesome opportunities that could come your way? Continue to plant the seed and fertilize accordingly and prepare to receive all God has in store for you.

10

Industries

Every industry has its purpose, whether essential or nonessential. One thing I notice with Christians is that we tend to stick to the same spaces, with ministry being the most common. Not that there is anything wrong with ministry being your primary source of work. But ministry is what we do no matter what industry we're in. We are needed everywhere but we need people of God to be dropped into a variety of industries.

It would be good to see the body of Christ more diversified and working in a variety of roles from therapists, artists, fashion designers, and even lawyers, just to name a few. I would also love to see us building more essential businesses. I believe in my heart that the God we serve has called His people to be diverse. We just can't be afraid to go where He is leading us. Sometimes God may lead us into spaces that don't seem like where we should be. Don't worry, it's all a part of His plan to set you on the path to your purpose. Remember, we are brilliant and have a lot to offer, so we don't want to keep our talents confined to one space.

As for industries, I've listed some below, with various roles falling into one or more of the following categories:

To Entertain – Movies, Sports, Comedy, Music, Social Media

To Inform – News, Magazines, Books, Social Media, Google

To Inspire – Churches, Mentors, Musicians, Singers, Motivational Speakers

To Help – Doctors, Lawyers, Therapists, Churches,

Volunteer Organizations, Politics

To Heal – Doctors, Churches, Therapists

To Teach and Train – Teachers, Coaches,
Personal Trainers

To Feed – Grocery Stores, Restaurants, Food Delivery

To Clothe – Retail, Fashion Designers, Textile

To Travel/Mobility – Airlines, Car Dealerships,
Rideshare, Travel Agencies, Public Transit

To House – Real Estate Agencies, Investors, Builders

To Finance – Banks, Credit Unions, Venture
Capitalists, Loan Companies, Investors

All of these industries serve our fellow man and are useful to society. They serve a purpose to make life better for all of us. We could use more Christians in every single one of them! For the remainder of this chapter, I'm going to outline some industries that I believe Christians can especially thrive in and where our brilliance can be put on full display.

THERAPY

As people of God, it's our duty to be of service to others in whatever form we can. With that said, if there is ever an industry where we could use more believers, it's therapy. If there is ever a place where someone could do God's work it's here. Any profession that offers mental support is a place where believers should consider a career. There is such a huge need. Although you may not always be able to directly share your beliefs with your patients, just the fact that you can bring the believing spirit with you into sessions would be an added bonus. In some cases, you can apply biblical principles at the patient's request, so consider stating that on your profile.

There is such a thing as faith-based counseling, I know of a few counselors who practice this way. One, in particular, is the creator of the "In The Light"

Any profession that offers mental support is a place where believers should consider a career.

podcast, a trauma therapist, Dr. Anita Phillips. She has most certainly made a name for herself in the faith-based counseling arena. Dr. Anita is known for her paradigm-shifting insights at the intersection of mental health, spirituality, and culture.[37]

She is trusted by a number of credible sources, which include "Essence," "The Talk," and "Tamron Hall," just to name a few. She is a trusted, faith-based, licensed mental health professional and, most importantly, God-fearing. I invite you to check her out.

There are many creative ways you could combine ministry with therapy. I know of a minister who merges her ministry with her practice beautifully. She is a licensed life coach, minister, and drug counselor who has a degree in discipleship. She uses her clinical skills and ministry to help heal others. She is a beautiful soul. If you feel you have been called into this type of role, this is one way you can operate in it. The world is definitely in need of more Christian counselors. I would recommend setting up your social media and branding to reflect that you are a faith-based counselor. You could start your own practice or you can always partner with churches and different ministries. Therapists are superheroes in my book, and we need more God-fearing believers in this role.

Tech

I'm starting to see a lot more godly influence in tech, and I must say I really like what I am seeing! There are tons of faith-based apps out there. Here are a few of my favorites.

Abide is a Christian meditation app. This app presents meditation from a biblical perspective with calming nature sounds and guided meditations that include Scripture readings. I've used it before, and it's a beautiful tool to include in your daily routine.

The Christian networking app Sprinkle of Jesus was created by well-known and beloved Instagram influencers Dana Chanel and Prince Donnell. It includes a wealth of resources of sermons from pastors around the world, courses, books, devotionals, and so much more. It's the perfect app to connect you with tons of faith-based resources and a community that is God-focused.

RightNow Media is one of the best platforms for pastors and church leaders to help properly equip their churches with the resources they need to stay connected with the Kingdom and with each other. It's a streaming library that features thousands of biblical resources with a user-friendly design and feature-rich application that makes it easy to consume content.

There is an app called Givlify, which is a giving app that allows you to tithe and give offerings electronically. Then, of course, there is the Bible app, along with other related apps like Word Alert, Verse of the Day, and Study Bible apps.

Even though there are tons of faith-based apps out there, we could still use more Christians in the world of tech. Especially because this is an industry where hardly any believers inhabit. I encourage Christians not to be afraid to go the tech route. A career in tech could be very rewarding and, most importantly, could do a lot to assist the church.

FASHION

I love the things I've been seeing in faith-based apparel. Some of the few that I follow are Art of Homage, 316Collection, and one of the more luxury brands, Fear of God. If you are heading into the fashion route, these brands are a fabulous point of reference. They have t-shirts, hoodies, hats, jackets—all embroidered with a clear message that God is their foundation. Take Fear of God luxury clothing, launched in 2013 by Jerry Lorenzo. The name of his label was inspired by his Christian faith and reading Oswald Chambers' devotional *My Utmost for His Highest,* which he read with his family as a child. This is a fabulous example of someone who infused his faith with fashion and was able to build a multi-million-dollar luxury brand out of it.

You can do such things too. If you choose this route, remember 1 Corinthians 10:31. Keep in mind that whoever is wearing your clothes is a walking advertisement, an ambassador for your brand. You are an ambassador for Christ, so be sure to use your creativity with respect to that.

ARCHITECTURE: CITY PLANNING

Look around you. Every building you see—apartments, homes, shopping complexes, hotels—all started on the drawing table somewhere. I don't know much about architecture, other than living in Toronto. I love looking at all the high rises outlined with mom-and-pop shops, thinking, "Wow, these started as someone's idea!" This industry presents a wide range of opportunities for designers, contractors, and all types of trades.

Christians can make an enormous impact on architecture and city planning. It's not just about building churches but the communities where those churches serve. Imagine the change you can make in underserved communities! Growing up in Cleveland, I saw the potential and still do. There is just no one willing to invest in the community. Let's say you are that someone, an architect with the skills and the funds to do it. Maybe you work for an architecture firm, or you started your own and have this passion to revive communities. I would tell you to first decide on what can benefit the people living there.

It's not just about building churches but the communities where those churches serve.

The first benefit would be to purchase and tear down all the abandoned buildings. In Cleveland, there are plenty. This would eliminate the possibility of them being used inappropriately, helping to eliminate the crime problem as well. A great example is a renovation of an old shopping mall in a suburb outside of Cleveland that is being turned into a mixed-use shopping complex. It's going to include a variety of clothing stores, restaurants, a movie theatre, and luxury apartments. This suburb also has a new high school being built, so combined with the mixed-use project, this will not only increase the property value in this suburb but the quality of life in that community as well.

Next would be to fix the streets. I don't know about you, but there are some places I automatically avoid because the streets are in such bad shape. I know I will need something fixed on my car later if I take that road. Street development is a big part of city planning because it determines whether people travel that road and, in some cases, whether or not businesses thrive. Most people avoid visiting places that are difficult to get to.

'Let's continue to brainstorm ideas to make the church the go-to place for the community.

❖

Now this all may sound very expensive, but it doesn't have to be done at once. Plus, efforts to improve the city are the type of thing that gets put on ballots during elections. Christians should certainly consider a career in city planning and/or architecture because of the advantage we would have being involved in creating the foundation in our communities. The foundation is the most important part, and if more of us are there, our communities would be in a much better position. Yes, this could get tricky because there are always politics involved with city planning, but the advantage we have if we are obedient Christians is that we would be able to discern situations better than most people.

This kind of profession may seem kind of intimidating, but we have the Holy Spirit as another tool in our toolbelt. Remember that when you feel discouraged. God will lead you to the resources you need to complete any project. As a God-fearing Christian Architect or city planner, you will have the best interest of the people and your integrity wouldn't be questioned. Some people may try you, but that happens no matter who you are. You would help build things that suit the needs of that community. You will help build up communities. Start small, learn how to draw up floor plans first, then expand to drawing up neighborhoods. Finally, learn how to create models when you get advanced enough. Get in touch with a city planner to see what plans they have for the city, if any, and go from there.

The Church

How do we use our skillsets to help the local church? There is much work to be done here, but primarily I want to discuss ways we can help churches enhance their ministry. I've grown up in the church, so I am very familiar with church culture. I understand why technology has always been an afterthought. A lot of churches are evolving, but most are still operating like they're in the 60s. There is this fear of technology taking the place of the sanctuary, but if you do it right, it can actually help fill it. Technology has given us a huge advantage (as we are seeing with online churches during the pandemic), and more churches should take advantage of it. Whatever it takes to save souls, I believe is worth it. This is one of the reasons why we need more millennials and younger people to find a church home because, for the most part, they are the ones who have the tech skills needed to help advance the church. Additionally, the pandemic won't last forever, so using the technology now can help advance the church later.

One way to utilize technology in the church is, of course, through social media. Take pictures, post quotes, and maybe even hire a professional photographer for church events. If possible, hire a social media manager. I've even seen some sponsored ads for churches on social media not selling anything but just advertising their ministry. If we can do it for our businesses, then we can do it for the church. With years of marketing experience, I believe that marketing is something a lot of churches could use help with. If you have marketing experience, I encourage you to bring your skillsets to the church. As a matter of fact, we all should be lending our talents and abilities to help the church. After all, the church is supposed to be a pillar in our community, right? What programs and events do we need in the church? I always thought networking events were a great thing to do within the church walls. I know of a few churches that have done this and have been very successful. There are a lot of ministry outreach programs, but how about a job fair, resume workshops, or coaching sessions? The church needs to start pulling in some of the talents from the community more often. No need to rent out an expensive venue, just do it within the church walls if possible. Let's continue to brainstorm ideas to make the church the go-to place for the community. We also need to do this because more and more of the younger generations are leaving the church.

This is not going to sound nice at all, but the older members won't always be around. *What will we do if the younger ones stop showing up? Who will carry on the church's legacy?* Developing programs and events and using technology should be a focus in order to reach and retain people, especially the youth in the community. Some churches, in my experience, do a good job at incorporating technology and a variety of appropriate resources, making it a great resource for the community and a great place to worship.

All of this, of course, is not an overnight process. These are just examples of how we could utilize our skills to assist the church in further influencing the environment.

It's a good thing to spread ourselves among different industries. Doing so benefits the church, blesses the world, and especially blesses the body of Christ. First Corinthians 3:9 (ESV) says, "For we are God's fellow workers; you are God's field, you are God's building." We are God's co-workers. We are working for Him and *with Him,* using our skills and talents to sow the Gospel.

If the rest of the world can work wonders, just imagine what you could do with your heavenly Father standing behind you? We can do exceedingly, abundantly more than we can ever ask for or imagine, just like He said, so, don't be afraid to pursue opportunities that may not seem like the status quo (Ephesians 3:20–21). No matter what industry you choose, trust that God has a plan for it.

11

Newness

"Forget the former things; do not dwell on the past. See, I am doing a new thing! Now it springs up; do you not perceive it? I am making a way in the wilderness and streams in the wasteland."

Isaiah 43:18–19 NIV

I've always been attracted to all things new—new beginnings, new scenery, new friendships, new things, that new car smell, the whole newish feeling. I guess you can say I'm attracted to *newness*. I have always craved new experiences and turning over new leaves because it all feels so refreshing. There's something about having something new. It gives me something to look forward to. We all want something new, don't we?

In today's world, we get bored so quickly and are ready to move on. There's nothing like a fresh start, right? Sadly, we do this with people too; I know I have. Hang out with a person a few times, then never call them again. People, like things, are replaceable these days. But what happens when newness becomes an addiction? It was always the same thing with me. "I can't wait to find a new job!" Or, "I can't wait to move!"; "I can't wait for this!"; "I can't wait for that!" So guess what happened? I never waited. I jumped ship every time I felt like I couldn't handle something or every time I got bored.

Newness entices me.

This chapter is for anybody addicted to newness, for anyone who is always searching for the next best thing. I never saw this as a problem until recently. Isaiah 43:18–19 tells of the prophet Isaiah writing to God's people during their captivity in Babylon. He was trying to remind them of who God is and what He did to free them from the Egyptians. This new thing the Lord was going to do for them would be even better than what He had done before. Let's take a closer look at these verses.

What sticks out for me is the part where it says, "now it springs forth; do you not perceive it?" This is Isaiah trying to convince his readers on a personal level what God is trying to convince us of. Why aren't we convinced that things will get better? Furthermore, why aren't we convinced that God's plans are better than our own? We are impatient people and want to jump to the conclusion that we think we know what is best for us. For those starting a new beginning, cheers! This could be good for you.

Yet, I'm willing to bet my life that the new thing God is doing for you is better than your new thing.

Toronto

When my husband and I first moved to Toronto, I thought all of my problems would immediately disappear. I couldn't wait to leave Cleveland. More importantly, I couldn't wait to start over. I took a risk and left my cushy job at a well-known hospital to make the move. I had benefits, decent pay, and there were tons of opportunities, but I still gave my two weeks' notice. A fresh new start in not just a new city but a whole new country couldn't have been more exciting to me. We had been preparing for this move for years, and it was finally happening. If you've never been to Toronto, let me tell you why it was so exciting for us. Toronto is like New York but safer and smaller. There is always something to do, tons of restaurants, bars, clubs, all the things that would entice most people. Pretty much, there is never a dull moment.

We found a new apartment, I got a new job that allowed me to work remotely, and just like that, we got a whole new beginning. Living in a high rise in a big city where you are within walking distance to everything was a huge step up from Cleveland, a much smaller city with far fewer resources and amenities. I thought, "This is it!" For anyone who has ever turned over a new leaf, you know the feeling. You feel like it solves all your problems. I got a new education, went back to school, and got my post-grad degree. Then I got a new job working in my field of study almost immediately after, and just like that, I was living my dream. I made new friends, traveled to new places, and I lived in a city where I never got bored. I had a whole new life. I would say I even had

If God was doing something new in my life, I would never see it because I wasn't patient enough to stick things out.

a second childhood. But, boy, was I in for a surprise, because well, *I still had the same issues.* Even moving to a whole new country didn't solve them—it just delayed them. It was more like a band-aid over my issue of never being satisfied personally and professionally. If God was doing something new in my life, I would never see it because I wasn't patient enough to stick things out.

Sadly, this impatient habit followed me to Toronto, as well as all my old debts. Bills needed to be paid and my student loans weren't going away, so I just kept pursuing money over my purpose. I would start over, jump to a new job, never finish a project, repeat, never allowing myself to see what new thing God was doing. This is what happens when you refuse to see the bigger picture. You end up right back where you started no matter where you move to.

I was addicted to whatever new thing I could start to get me out of whatever situation I didn't like. It was my escape plan. I was never satisfied, so even after only two years of living in our new apartment, I was ready to move again.

Just like a new car has that fresh new car smell so does new life experiences. However, once that new car smell is gone, you just don't go out and buy a new car, right? Of course not. Had I pursued the right opportunities in the first place, this and many other books would have been written years ago.

Sadly, a lot of the projects God had in mind for me never happened because I couldn't get over my addiction to always want something new. Early on in my life, it was the absolute worst. I changed jobs frequently. The longest I stayed was maybe three years. I had the same problem with my education. I changed majors several times and attended multiple colleges to the point that I had exhausted all of my federal aid and student loans. The amount of debt I put myself in was incomprehensible.

This was also a problem when it came to relationships too. I always had the awful habit of ending relationships prematurely, whether it was a personal

God's new is different from our new.

or professional relationship. After a month of getting to know someone, I would talk myself out of building anything further with them out of fear of what would happen if I let my guard down. Vulnerability scared me. I would say things to myself like, "What do they like about me?" "Hmm, why didn't they text back?" I would find a reason to think they were acting funny, then after that, the relationship would fade. I would lose them, and they would lose me. Nothing lasted with me because I was always seeking something new to make up for what I thought I didn't have. I thought something new would always make things better, but *God's new is different from our new*. With our new, we are always chasing freedom, money, and people. With God's new, it's about more than earthly things. After a while, I started hearing a voice say, "Maria, God is doing a new thing, you just have to allow Him to do it."

If you're like me, you've got to learn to be patient and trust the process, because if you don't, you'll just keep staying in this hamster wheel. When there's no progression in your life, you have to ask yourself, "What's stopping me?" I hate to break it to you but *it's probably you*. You are in the way. God is trying to do a new thing, but you won't let Him.

Walking in your purpose requires commitment and obedience, something I know is not easy, but you have to try. Sometimes you may have to pivot, leave a job, move, change directions in some way, but make sure you are doing it for the right reasons. Make sure it all fits into your big picture. My problem is I never did it for the right reasons. I felt like all would be right with the world if I simply changed jobs or moved, but that's not how things work. While I was going through my transitions, I never inserted anything that had anything to do with writing. Didn't read many books, never joined any writing groups, never sought mentorship, and, most disappointing, I barely wrote anything. I didn't take writing seriously at all. I had blogs I would abandon and half-written manuscripts. How could I say I wanted to have this prosperous writing career and never write? Because I was chasing freedom and money instead of purpose.

God had so much in store for me as a writer and so much in store for my life period, but I wouldn't allow myself to see it. Chasing worldly goals instead of purpose won't get you far—trust me.

The New Thing

What is this new thing that God is doing? There are three parts to it—the spiritual, the mental, and the physical. When God is doing something, He includes all three, but you must possess the most important fruit of all to see it—faith.

The Spiritual

God is not a man. He does not operate like us. He can manage and manifest an infinite number of things all at once. We get tired and weary, while He never tires. We worry and get frustrated, while He remains unbothered. God remains faithful, while we continuously jump ship. If you have faith, you will go through a period of immense growth. I got saved several years ago, let's say around my mid-twenties. After that, when I had my first encounter with the Holy Spirit, there was a spiritual awakening that happened. I was born again, the spiritual part of the new thing. The Holy Spirit has been instrumental in increasing my discernment, providing guidance, wisdom, and comfort, and He will do the same for you. If you are headed in the wrong direction and you have the Holy Spirit, you better believe He will let you know. He will convict you, not condemn you—there's a difference.

The Mental

God mentally helps you become more at peace with your decisions. This is how you know you are going in the right direction. With His Holy Spirit, He may navigate you toward resources which can be in the form of books, media, scriptures, things you read or hear from others that confirm you are on the right path. You may be led toward certain Scriptures that give you pause in relating to your specific situation. He will use other believers and those closest to you to encourage and support you, to confirm you are doing what you should be doing.

The Physical

The physical part is the opportunities that are divinely ordained. Have you ever had an opportunity just come out of the blue? This is where you combine your faith with your works so that the physical can manifest. If you've made it to the physical and remain obedient, this new thing God is doing has His favor written all over it.

When you allow yourself to see the bigger picture, you can see what God is doing more clearly. What has helped me to see this picture better is investing in myself. Investing in yourself is how you "actively wait" on the Lord. I surround myself with people who have similar aspirations to me. I read more so I'm learning and growing more. Now, I've finally secured my career as a full-time writer. I am pouring into myself as much as possible, and I'm beginning to see this new thing evolve. As with any growth period, it's not without its adversities. Of course, I have made some mistakes along the way. I learned that success is a combination of wins and losses. Just stay the course, be obedient, and don't be so quick to jump ship like I always did. Sometimes you have to ask yourself, "Do I just want the lifestyle or do I want my purpose? Am I willing to wait for the new thing?" Let me tell you, this new thing God is doing in your life is *so* worth the wait if you just hang in there!

12

Checkmate.

HERE WE ARE, YOU MADE IT!

By now, I hope that you understand your role, that it's not all about you, and the details do matter. How you walk, talk, how you treat people, the company you keep—it all matters. There is someone out there who is tied to your gift. No matter what you do or who you are, you've got something special that someone needs. I hope you understand why obedience should not be an afterthought, and most importantly, I hope you learn to be led by the Spirit and not the world. When God gives you a gift, He expects you to use it appropriately. Someone out there needs your gift, so you need to be ready and be equipped with the right stuff. Empowerment is great and self-help is helpful, but know this: *You are not just dealing with the physical; you are also dealing with the spiritual.* Some people are more susceptible to being misled so, my loves, we have to be careful what we are pouring into people by watching who we allow to pour into us. In some way or another, we are all students who eventually become teachers and vice versa.

Above all, your gifts, business, brand, skills—everything has its purpose in God's Kingdom. Our gifts, skills, and talents can work anywhere and are applicable in any industry, remember that. We must all accept that we are managers and not owners. This is a hard reality to face, but at the end of the day, it's about serving God. No matter what you are building, God must be woven into the foundation first. Be smart and practice discernment. You can't work with everyone and you can't go where everyone else is going. Spend time with God daily and allow *Him* to reveal Himself to you. There have been times when God would reveal Himself to me, whether I was looking for Him or not. It didn't matter if I didn't want to be found, He would find me.

*The best advice I could give you is to not let the
world shape your view of who God really is.*

The best advice I could give you is to not let the world shape your view of who God really is. For a reminder of what spending time with God looks like, here are examples from chapter 8 on obedience:

◊ Get your daily Word in. One of my favorite books in the Bible is the book of Proverbs.

◊ Fast as often as you can. I fast once a week. Fasting is a powerful tool and an even more powerful weapon against the enemy.

◊ Spend time with God in prayer, and He will lead you to the resources that are more suited for you. Ultimately, He will lead you back to Him.

Practice these disciplines, in addition to attending church, Bible study, all of the things you should be doing, and you will build up your discernment and avoid distractions—"Go this way, that way, no this way is better." I've come to know that there is only one way—God's way. Let Him show you the way you should go (Psalm 32:8). Give Him a chance—hasn't He done the most for you anyway? Lots of people want what God can give them, but they don't want Him. But the Bible tells us, "Seek first the kingdom of God and his righteousness, and all these things will be added to you" (Matthew 6:33 ESV).

Seek Him first, then make your move.

Playing Chess with God

In an art gallery in London hangs a painting of a chess game entitled "The Chess Players." On one side of the chessboard is the devil, full of laughter. His hand is poised, ready to make the next move. On the other side of the chessboard sits a shaking, frightened young man. Sweat drips down his forehead mixed with tears pouring from his eyes.

One day, a chess champion from another country visited the gallery. The painting naturally caught his attention causing him to examine it for a very long time. In fact, while others had moved on throughout the gallery, the chess champion remained fixated on the game and the devil who was about to make the next move to steal this man's soul.

Hours passed as the chess champion continued to study the board from every possible angle. The sweat on the young man's face begged him to continue. Finally, as the gallery was about to close for the night, people in every part of the enormous building heard a loud scream as the chess champion yelled, "Yes! I've got it! You don't have to lose!"

What this chess champion had done was discover another move that the man could take. He had found a way not only for the young man to escape checkmate, but to deliver checkmate on the devil only a few more moves into the game.[38]

When I look at this story, instead of the devil playing chess, let's put the world in its place. The world plays chess in a lot of ways, using trends, politics, and New Age beliefs to make moves. It can feel intimidating, and it often looks like the world will win. But God always has another move. He has the final move. Do you want to know what your move is? Your purpose—that's your move. You will always win because God is behind your purpose. He is the Author and the Finisher. The victory is already yours—you just have to make your first move. Put down all your idols, stand firm, and make room for your purpose. And remember to always keep God in the details.

Acknowledgments

LADY KRISTA VARNADO, ED.D. KINGDOM WOMEN ACTIVATED (KWA):
OAKWOOD BIBLE FELLOWSHIP

I was looking for more support with my Bible studies, a more personal connection, so I sought out a small group. I had been tuning in to my normal Bible studies at my church, however, I had a desire to connect with the body of Christ in a more personal way, which meant a smaller group of people. During the pandemic, that desire became even stronger. I was also living out of the country at the time away from organic connections, like friends and family and my church, so I felt very much alone. I had been tuning into Dr. Tony Evans' OCBF Broadcast on YouTube and listening to his podcasts for a while, so naturally, I looked to OCBF to find a small group. I reached out to Krista Varnado who was the virtual small group leader for Oakwood Bible Fellowship. Krista's dedication to the small group and her interest in my spiritual growth in Christ was instrumental in the success of writing this book. I eventually sought Krista out for help using her years of experience in academia. She provided stellar coaching and editing for some of the most pivotal chapters in my book. Perhaps the most helpful part of coaching was the encouragement I received when I felt tired and attacked. I am so glad to have found such a monumental resource in my spiritual journey and have met some wonderful women of God along the way. Sister Krista, there were times I felt so overwhelmed and attacked, but your dedication and encouragement gave me the motivation I needed to stay the course. Thank you so much. God bless!

My husband, Christopher Tolliver

To my love, my husband, and my best friend, Christopher. Words cannot express how much you mean to me. I could write a million love letters and they still wouldn't express how much I love you. You are my best friend, biggest supporter, biggest cheerleader, and I am yours. Even though you may not be able to relate to some of the content in this book, you understood that writing a book is no easy task and you made sure I was able to get every resource I needed to make sure it was successful. You knew how important this book was to me and that's all you needed to know to support me. Whatever I needed you never hesitated to help. You are and have always been there for me. You are an amazing husband, father, friend, brother, son—an amazing person all the way around. Thank you for being everything I need in a husband and friend. Love you a million times infinity!

Notes

Are You Called?

1 Pastor Tony Evans, "The Motivation of Kingdom Stewardship." Tony Evans: The Urban Alternative; https://store.tonyevans.org/purchase/the-motivation-of-kingdom-stewardship-dvd, 2020.

Chapter 1: Idols

2 Pastor Tony Evans, Twitter, @drtonyevans, September 15, 2020.

3 American Society of Plastic Surgeons, "Plastic Surgery Statistics Report: ASPS National Clearinghouse of Plastic Surgery Procedural Statistics 2020"; https://www.plasticsurgery.org/documents/News/Statistics/2020/plastic-surgery-statistics-full-report-2020.pdf.

4 "Revenue of the cosmetic and beauty industry in the United States from 2002 to 2020 (in billion U.S. dollars)," Published by M. Ridder, Statista, November 24, 2020; https://www.statista.com/statistics/243742/revenue-of-the-cosmetic-industry-in-the-us/.

5 Stephanetta (isis) Harmon, "Black Consumers Spend Nine Times in Hair & Beauty: Report," February 26, 2018; https://www.hypehair.com/86642/black-consumers-continue-to-spend-nine-times-more-in-beauty-report/.

6 Idol. https://www.merriam-webster.com/dictionary/idol.

Chapter 2: The Freedom Trap

7 Steward. https://www.dictionary.com/browse/steward.

Chapter 3: Bad Advice

[8] Hame@BIH, "Denzel Washington—About the Fake News" (2016); https://www.youtube.com/watch?v=U3pV_Mw4mrM, June 2, 2020.

[9] Conform. https://www.oxfordlearnersdictionaries.com/definition/american_english/conform.

[10] Transform. https://www.merriam-webster.com/dictionary/transform.

Section 2: Build

[11] Build. https://www.merriam-webster.com/dictionary/build.

Chapter 4: The Process of Elimination

[12] Eliminate. https://www.dictionary.com/browse/eliminate.

[13] Erika Anderson, "21 Quotes From Henry Ford On Business, Leadership And Life," Forbes.com, May 21, 2013; https://www.forbes.com/sites/erikaandersen/2013/05/31/21-quotes-from-henry-ford-on-business-leadership-and-life/?sh=1ebd932f293c.

Chapter 5: Follow-Unfollow

[14] Jeannie Ortega Law, "Former Victoria's Secret model who gave up career for Jesus produces faith-based film," CP Entertainment, September 14, 2019; https://www.christianpost.com/news/former-victorias-secret-model-who-gave-up-career-for-jesus-produces-faith-based-film.html.

Chapter 6: Competition

[15] Lemelson-MIT; https://lemelson.mit.edu/resources/marie-van-brittan-brown; also, Njera Perkins, "Meet Marie Van Brittan Brown, the Nurse Turned Inventor Behind the First Home Security System," Afrotech, Technology, February 18, 2021; https://afrotech.com/meet-marie-van-brittan-brown-the-nurse-turned-inventor-behind-the-first-home-security-system.

[16] Brilliant. https://www.merriam-webster.com/dictionary/brilliant.

[17] Meredith Worthen, "Alice Ball Biography (1892–1916)," March 1, 2018; https://www.biography.com/scientist/alice-ball.

[18] Mae C. Jemison Biography (1956-), April 2, 2014; https://www.

biography.com/astronaut/mae-c-jemison?li_source=LI&li_medium=m2m-rcw-biography; also, Alexander, Kerri Lee. "Mae Jemison." National Women's History Museum. 2019. www.womenshistory.org/education-resources/biographies/mae-jemison.

[19] Changing the Face of Medicine, "Dr. Virginia Apgar Biography," 2015, National Institutes of Health, https://cfmedicine.nlm.nih.gov/physicians/biography_12.html.

[20] "Patricia Bath Biography," A&E Television Networks, April 2, 2014, last updated January 7, 2021; https://www.biography.com/scientist/patricia-bath; Changing the Face of Medicine, Patricia Bath Biography, 2003, National Institutes of Health, https://cfmedicine.nlm.nih.gov/physicians/biography_26.html.

Chapter 7: Clarifying Your Mission

[21] Arrogance. https://www.collinsdictionary.com/dictionary/english-thesaurus/self-important.

Chapter 8: Obedience

[22] Obedience. https://www.lexico.com/definition/obedience.

[23] Compliance. https://www.lexico.com/en/definition/compliance.

[24] Christianity Today 2018, "Looking for Ancient African Religion? Try Christianity." The United Nations, accessed 18 January 2018; https://www.christianitytoday.com/ct/2018/january-web-only/urban-christianity-ancient-africa-apologetics.html.

[25] Pastor Tony Evans, One Place; https://www.oneplace.com/ministries/the-alternative/.

[26] Pastor Tony Evans, "CBS Tony Evans Study Bible," (Nashville: Holman Bible Publishers, 2017).

Chapter 9: Marketing

[27] Matt Ellis, "Branding colors: Everything you need to choose your brand's color palette"; https://99designs.ca/blog/tips/branding-colors/.

[28] Morgan Anglin, "Choosing the best social media platform for your nonprofit," DotOrg Solutions, May 20, 2021; https://blog.dotorgsolutions.com/blog/choosing-the-best-social-media-platform-for-your-nonprofit.

[29] "8 Massive Benefits of Using YouTube For Business," Grow: Small Business Marketing Experts; https://wearegrow.com/8-massive-benefits-of-using-youtube-for-business/

[30] "8 Massive Benefits of Using YouTube For Business," Grow: Small Business Marketing Experts; https://wearegrow.com/8-massive-benefits-of-using-youtube-for-business/.

[31] "8 Massive Benefits of Using YouTube For Business," Grow: Small Business Marketing Experts; https://wearegrow.com/8-massive-benefits-of-using-youtube-for-business/.

[32] "Distribution of Twitter users worldwide as of April 2021, by age group," Statista; https://www.statista.com/statistics/283119/age-distribution-of-global-twitter-users/

[33] Nathan Thomas, "8 Best Social Media Platforms for Business: Your Ultimate Guide," Optinmaster, March 15, 2021; https://optinmonster.com/best-social-media-platforms-for-business/#fb.

[34] Chris Pemberton, "Tap into the marketing power of SMS," Gartner, November 3, 2016; https://www.gartner.com/en/marketing/insights/articles/tap-into-the-marketing-power-of-sms.

[35] Jake Jeffries, "Email Marketing VS SMS Marketing the Stats [Infographic]," B2C, February 26, 2018; https://www.business2community.com/infographics/email-marketing-vs-sms-marketing-stats-infographic-02021390.

[36] L. Ceci, "WhatsApp usage penetration in the United States 2020, by age group," Statista, January 6, 2022; https://www.statista.com/statistics/814649/whatsapp-users-in-the-united-states-by-age/.

Chapter 10: Industries

[37] https://www.anitaphillips.com/.

Chapter 12: Checkmate

[38] Pastor Tony Evans, "Checkmating Satan," The Alternative View, 2020. Tony Evans: The Urban Alternative; https://tonyevans.org/august-2017-checkmating-satan.

About the Author

A formally trained writer and digital marketer, Maria Tolliver has worked in the digital marketing industry for over six years. She has worked in almost every creative form of digital marketing, from copywriting and graphic design, to designing websites, social media management, and ghostwriting for aspiring authors. Born and raised in humble beginnings in the inner city of Cleveland, Ohio, Maria is no stranger to hard work and getting creative to make things work. Her strong desire to work in creative industries, such as film and tv production, led her to the film and digital media program at Cleveland State University where she obtained her bachelor's degree. Her most memorable class was a screenwriting course that enhanced her storytelling skills and increased her interest in the craft. Out of that, her passion for writing grew into a variety of creative avenues.

Maria's love for writing didn't start there. She began her writing career journaling, then over the years grew into writing poetry, songs, screenwriting, blogging, and eventually securing a career as a copywriter and freelance writer. Maria and her husband, Chris, relocated out of the country for a few years to Toronto, Ontario, where she obtained her master's degree in Interactive Media Management, a specialized digital marketing program at Centennial College where she graduated with honors. From there, she secured multiple opportunities in her field of study, made many valuable connections, and wrote her first book *God in the Details*. Now residing in South Euclid, Ohio, Maria lives with her husband and their daughter, Jada, and plans to create more inspiring content for years to come. For more about Maria, visit mariatolliver.com.